MICRO CREDIT MANAGEMENT BY WOMEN'S SELF-HELP GROUPS

MICRO CREDIT MANAGEMENT BY WOMEN'S SELF-HELP GROUPS

By

Dr. U. Jerinabi
Reader in Commerce
Avinashilingam Deemed University
Coimbatore–641 043

DISCOVERY PUBLISHING HOUSE
NEW DELHI-110002

First Published-2006
Reprinted: 2013
ISBN 81-8356-111-X

Published by

DISCOVERY PUBLISHING HOUSE
4831/24, Ansari Road, Prahlad Street,
Darya Ganj, New Delhi-110002 (India)
Phone: 23279245 • Fax: 91-11-23253475
E-mail:dphtemp@indiatimes.com

Printed at:
Dynamic printers, Delhi

Preface

India has a population exceeding 1027.01 million, with 742 million living in rural areas. About 40 per cent of India's population are poor; 23.62 per cent of the urban population and 27.09 per cent of the rural population are estimated to be living below the poverty line. The major causes of poverty are lack of access to and control over resources. The poor have little saving and have to rely on borrowings to meet their consumption and production needs. Credit plays a crucial role in the economy of poor households.

Women as micro and small entrepreneurs have increasingly become a key target group for micro-credit programme. Providing access to micro-credit is considered a precondition for poverty alleviation, but also for women's empowerment. As poor women are increasingly recognised to be better borrowers, they are starting to become of interest also to regular financial institutions. But despite the proven positive impact entrepreneurs in the informal sector, micro-finance is just one pool among others to address the multiple causes of poverty, unemployment and social exclusion.

Self Help Groups (SHGs) form the basic constituent unit of the micro-credit movement in India. An SHG is a group of a few individuals—usually poor and often women—who pool their savings into a fund from which they can borrow as and when they can borrow as and when necessary. Such a group is linked with a rural bank, co-operative or commercial bank where they maintain a group account. Most of the NGOs have been previously functioning in different developmental roles among the poor, and now added micro-credit to the list of services they provided. A few others, impressed by the success of micro-finance elsewhere, started off as MFIs. Self Help Groups (SHGs) among the poor mostly women, have rapidly become a common rural phenomenon in many Indian states. NGOs provide the leadership and management necessary informing and running such groups in most cases.

This action research concentrates on the study of micro-credit management by the women's Self Help Groups (SHGs). The main objectives of the study were to form SHGs in the rural and urban areas and to study the impact of the efforts on the SHGs in qualitative and quantitative dimensions. The findings of the study would enable the government, financing agents and the NGO's to frame policies and to co-ordinate their activities and exchange their experiences in the area of micro-finance and gender and to allow for the participation of clients especially women entrepreneurs in the design and offering of financial services to micro and small enterprises.

—Author

Contents

1

Introduction

"Micro-credit is a critical antipoverty tool, a wise investment in human capital. When the poorest, especially women receive credit, they become economic actors with power to improve not only their own lives, but in a widening circle of impact, the lives of their families, their communities and their relations".

–Kofi Annan

Secretary General, United Nations

INTRODUCTION

India has a population of 1027.01 million with 742 million living in rural areas.[1] About 40 per cent of the rural population and 23.62 per cent of the urban population are estimated to be living below the poverty line.[2] The urban and rural poor have been dependent on moneylenders for their financial needs, such as marriage in the family, illness or other emergency needs, as the formal credit system of banks, by and large, is beyond the rich of the poor. This provides an opportunity for moneylenders to exploit the situation.

The prime need of the hour is to ensure that the poor live with dignity, sufficiency and responsibility. It is also recognised that the poor people are bankable and that they themselves are likely to have a better appreciation of their socio-economic situation. The activities of Self Help Groups (SHGs) have emerged as a sustainable approach to make credit facilities available to the poor at their door step in a simple and flexible manner.

SELF HELP GROUPS: EVOLUTION, CONCEPT AND FEATURES

(i) Evolution of SHGs

The genesis of SHGs could be traced to "Mutual Aid" in Indian village community. In traditional rural societies, self-help takes various forms. Activities like housing/farm operations, which have to be completed within stipulated time, depend upon such arrangements Likewise, people share implements required in agricultural production. Sharing of irrigation water/bullocks necessitates a management based on self-help. However, in the West, the theoretical approach to collective action was among others, developed by Olson and he says people will participate in collective action when they are organised in small groups when the expected private benefits from the collective action exceed the expected private costs of participation.[3]

The existence of traditional saving groups has been well documented and has a long and successful history in India. Informal SHGs oriented to saving and credit functions are not a new phenomenon.[4] Some forms of credit instruments were in operation even before 1904 when the Co-operative Credit Societies Act was passed. Credit instruments such as Nidhis and Chit Funds were popular, especially in South India. They had several distinguishing features, such as encouraging thrift, mobilising small savings and inculcating in the members the habits of punctuality and planning for future. The useful role played by these instruments in the rural areas as important sources of credit to people with moderate needs has been well recognised.

The SHG is defined as a voluntary group valuing personal interactions and mutual aid as a means of altering or ameliorating the problems perceived as alterable, pressing, and personal by most of its participants.[5] These groups are voluntary associations of people formed to attain certain collective goals that could be economic, social or both. They policy planners and development planners cherish the myth that poor people do not have the spirit to thrift, but recent reports from different parts of the globe challenge this.[6]

Since the SHGs in India are informal groups, their legal status has not been defined. What they initially intended was to bring together people, particularly economically weaker sections and to undertake activities of mutual interest. Members of SHGs have no risk taking ability, hardly anything to offer as guarantee against availing loans from formal Rural Financial Institutions (RFIs) and limited earning opportunities. However, thrift, credit and income generating activities emerged as the major activities of the SHGs. In other words, the SHGs evolved a system for collective savings, group consumption credit, as well as, integrating social and economic goals among small groups.

The initial growth of SHGs has been in areas where they received support from Non-Government Organisations (NGOs). The NGOs supported not only in the formation of SHGs but also in identifying economic activities, imparting training, and even financial support in the initial stage. The critical areas in forming the groups at the beginning were their size and composition, homogeneity, group discipline, saving habits and sustainability. By offering saving services, a financial institution can promote greater customer loyalty and loan repayment discipline, thus reducing the institutions's cost of funds for on-lending and overall transaction cost. Moreover, RFIs can also improve their viability by expanding their volume of business.[7] Subsequently, the SHGs have been linked with banks for saving and credit operations. Bank linkage model evolved as a core strategy that could be used by the banking system for increasing its outreach to the poorest of the poor who were hitherto getting by-passed by it.[8]

(ii) Concept of SHG

The Self Help Groups (SHGs) are voluntary associations of people formed to attain a collective goal. People who are homogeneous with respect to social background, heritage, caste or traditional occupation come together for a common cause to raise and manage resources for the benefit of the group members.

The process by which the group of people with a common objective are facilitated to come together in order to participate in the development activities i.e., savings, credit, income generation, etc., is called GROUP FORMATION.

Although the SHGs can be formed for any development activity, for the financial institutions to use them as a conduit for banking activities, the SHGs should be practising thrift and credit and be familiar with money management.[9]

(iii) Features of SHGs

Generally, SHGs encompass several activities of men and women but the Indian focus is on financial aspects of SHGs. In addition to India, this financial SHG concept is being promoted in Bangladesh, Indonesia, Thailand, Philippines, Nepal, Sri Lanka, etc. The salient features of SHGs are:

(i) Homogeneous in terms of economic status and interest and an affinity group.

(ii) Small in size and their membership per group range from 10 to 20 people.

(iii) They are non-political and voluntary and follow democratic culture.

(iv) They hold weekly meetings and mostly during non-working hours.

(v) They have the transparency among themselves and they have the collective accountability of financial transactions in the group.

(iv) Functions

(i) Conduct regular weekly meetings;

(ii) Promote saving attitude and habit among the members;

(iii) Indulge in credit management;

(iv) Build the common-fund slowly and systematically; and

(v) Establish linkage with bank and government department.

A typical SHG model is depicted in Figure 1.1. Some of the features might vary from one SHG to another promoted by various NGOs, banks, etc.

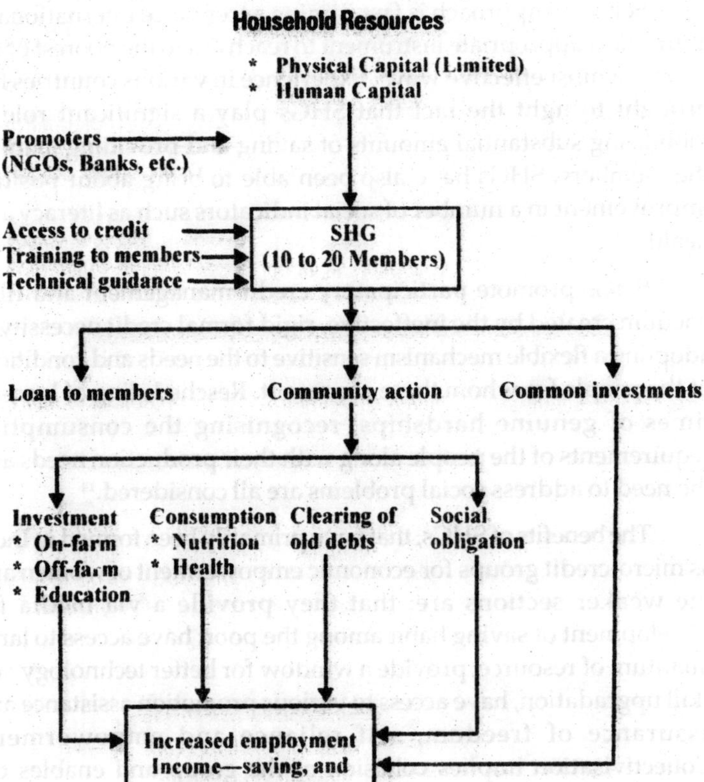

Fig. 1.1: A Typical SHG Model

(v) Significance of SHGs

SHGs are necessary to overcome exploitation, create confidence for economic self-reliance in the poor, particularly to women who are mostly invisible in the social structure. The SHGs become the basis 'for action and change' and build a relationship of mutual trust between the promoting organisation and the rural poor through constant contact and genuine efforts.[10] Credit delivery through thrift and credit groups (SHGs) emerges as an alternative to the existing system of credit disbursement by the banks. SHGs have been found to help inculcate among their members sound habits of thrift, saving and banking.[11]

Self-help approach is fast gaining acceptance internationally as the most appropriate instrument to reach out to the poorest of the poor in a most effective way.[12] Experience in various countries has brought to light the fact that SHGs play a significant role in mobilising substantial amounts of saving and providing loans to the members. SHGs have also been able to bring about positive improvement in a number of social indicators such as literacy and health.[13]

SHGs promote participatory credit management and fill a vacuum created by the ineffective, rigid formal credit necessity of adopting a flexible mechanism sensitive to the needs and conditions of the people for whom these are meant. Rescheduling of loans in times of genuine hardships, recognising the consumption requirements of the people along with their production needs and the need to address social problems are all considered.[14]

The benefits of SHGs, that have primarily been formed in India as micro-credit groups for economic empowerment of women and the weaker sections are: that they provide a via media for development of saving habit among the poor; have access to large quantum of resource; provide a window for better technology and skill upgradation, have access to various promotion assistance and assurance of freedom, self reliance and empowerment. Collectivisation implies cohesion of the group and enables the members of the group to perceive common interests and act collectively. In contrast to formal organisations, self-help is highly personal, non-hierarchical and without division of labour. Self-help favours experience over expertise.[15]

MICRO CREDIT—NEED AND EMERGENCE

The structure of rural financial market in India is dualistic consisting of both formal and informal financial intermediaries. A consensus is growing among researchers that the formal financial sector is not effectively serving the rural population in the Third World Countries.[16] This is mainly attributed to the failure of financial intermediaries in fulfilling their basic functions namely, production credit to finance income generating activities, consumption credit to maintain and expand human productive capacity and quality saving schemes for increasing risk bearing capacity of the rural households. Moreover, these institutions have failed to promote any of their social objectives.[17] To reach the poor, institutional innovations are needed that enable services to be expanded, while substantially reducing transaction costs for both financial institutions and clients.[18] In many countries in the world, micro-credit programmes have succeeded in generating self-employment by providing access to small capital to people living in poverty.[19]

The performance of formal financial institutions particularly in their lending to the poor in India has been unsatisfactory. They face a number of constraints in broadening their services to the poor. As a result of the inaccessibility of the formal banking system to the poor, micro-financial institutions emerged, which act as an impetus for community action.[20] There has been a surge of interest in micro-finance in the recent past, particularly in the context of reaching the poor families in a more effective way.[21] As an informal supplementary credit delivery mechanism by lending at a group level, the Self Help Groups (SHGs) came into existence.

Finance is basic to any economic activity. The basic philosophy of rural finance is the dispensation of loans at a concessional rate through administrative control targeting the rural people engaged either in agricultural or non-agricultural activities. But it is felt that a large number of poverty stricken people and particularly the women, who constitute a significant number, still remain outside the ambit of institutional finance. In order to give a new approach to rural finance. National Bank for Agricultural and Rural Development (NABARD) had introduced the 'Self Help Groups' in 1992 which is generally treated as finance to a small group. This new approach, in other words, is known as *Micro Credit*.

Micro-credit programmes extend small loans to poor people for self-employment projects that generate income, allowing them to care for themselves and their families. In most cases, micro-credit programmes offer a combination of services and resources to their clients in addition to credit for self-employment. These often include savings, training networking and peer support. It is ironical that micro enterprises are often unorganised, decentralised and unprotected and their contribution to the economy often remains unorganised.

In February 1997, a summit was convened in Washington to review and give direction for financing to the poorest people in the underdeveloped countries. The summit defined its goal to Micro-finance those "programmes that provide credit for self-employment and other financial and business services (including savings and other technical assistance) to very poor persons." Micro level financial schemes help people to help themselves by starting small income generation projects and activities.[22]

The maximum experimentation with micro-credit can be seen in Bangladesh, where it has been extensively used for reaching the poorest sections of the society. It has proved to be a most powerful weapon to fight poverty. During the seventies many initiatives were taken in developed and developing countries in Asia, Africa and Latin America. The approach of micro-credit consisted of Self Help Groups (SHGs), Revolving Savings and Credit Associations (ROSCAS), Solidarity Groups, Money Store, etc. Some of the examples outside India as Philippine Commercial and Industrial Bank, Rural Bank of Ghana and Grameen Bank (Bangladesh).[23] The Grameen Bank set up in 1976 by Muhammad Yunus, is one of the most popular models for providing micro-credit to poor. At present 90 per cent of the members are women.[24]

In India, Self Employment Women's Association (SEWA) in Gujarat and Madhya Pradesh, Mysore Resettlement Development Agency (MYRADA) in Karnataka, Professional Assistance for Development Action (PRADAN) in Rajasthan, Association of Sarva Seva Farms (ASSEFA) in Tamil Nadu, New Public School Society in Uttar Pradesh, and other organisations took up the initiative. The credit needs of groups are met in a convenient, flexible and cost-effective way.

NABARD's efforts of improving the access of the rural poor to formal banking services through SHGs has gathered momentum during the last few years. It not only extends 100 per cent refinance facilities to the banks at concessional interest rate, but it has also taken various promotional initiatives to expand SHG-Bank linkage programme.[25] Small Industries Development Bank of India (SIDBI) also extends credit facilities through NGOs and more than 150 NGOs had availed credit facilities from SIDBI for on-lending to small borrowers.[26]

The Department of Women and Child Development launched the Indira Mahila Yojana (IMY) in 1995 as a central sector project for the holistic empowerment of women in 200 blocks. Under this programme, efforts are being made for setting up of SHGs of women. IMY aims to fill up the gaps where suitable NGOs are not available to take up micro-credit programme.[27] Rashtriya Mahila Kosh (RMK) was set up in March 1993, with the objective of extending credit limits to poor women through NGOs. Women Development Corporations (WDC), Co-operative Societies and Indira Mahila Block Samitees and taking up other promotional and advocacy roles to achieve economic self reliance for women. Credit facilities are extended at eight per cent interest, which, in turn, is lent to SHGs at the interest rate of 12 per cent per annum. SHGs can lend to the women members at an interest rate not exceeding the State Bank of India (SBI) interest rate on unsecured advanced. NGOs can also extend loan facilities to individual women where SHGs do not exist.[28]

EMPOWERMENT OF WOMEN

The Global Conference on Women's Empowerment, 1988, highlighted Empowerment as the surest way of making women "partners in development". Development on the other hand should ultimately become a process of empowerment. Empowerment is an active process enabling women to realise their full identity and power in all spheres of life.

Although women form nearly half of the human capital in the country. They are still the most deprived and neglected segments of society despite the constitutional guarantee for equal rights and privileges for men and women. Women continue to be victims of a process of economic, social, cultural and political marginalisation. Women are viewed as homemakers and are not encouraged to undertake professions to which men have a natural access. On the other hand, half of the world's food is produced by women working in the fields and they constitute 1/3 of the world's labour force. Although woman does double the amount of work and contributes doubly to the economy, she is considered a burden and instances of female infanticide and foeticide bear testimony to this. Empowerment is a multifaceted process encompassing aspects such as enhancing awareness, increasing access to resources—economics, social and political. It comprises an equally important component of mobilisation and organisation of women into groups, because these groups form the basis for solidarity, strength and collective action.

Empowerment of women is a critical factor in the eradication of poverty, as the women are the key contributors to the economy and to combating poverty through both remunerative and unremunerative work at home, in the community and in the work place.[29] Gainful employment has been viewed as a critical entry point for women's integration in development.[30]

Women's participation in income generating activities is believed to increase their status and decision-making power. With employment women do not remain as 'objects' of social change but become 'agents' of it. They cease from being 'consumers' of economic goods and services and turn into 'producers'. They participate in social reproduction as well as reproduction of labour for the next generation.[31]

In many cases, micro-credit has been a crucial element in increasing women's economic opportunities. When done well, it gives women the ability to make a living on a sustainable basis. Micro-credit could unleash the economic potential of hundreds of millions of the world's poorest.

The country's response to the challenges of equality, development and peace is the "empowerment strategy". The challenge before the society is to evolve strategies to break the stereotypes of the past by solving problems of poverty, illiteracy, environmental degradation, violence, gender inequality, etc. Hence self-help groups and micro credit should be seen as components of a solution to accelerate the socio-economic development particularly, of the rural poor women in India. A judicious mix of Macro Credit along with other activities with emphasis on development and empowerment strategies and processes would certainly make Micro Credit an effective instrument of social and economic development particularly, of women in a holistic and integrated manner.[32]

In the light of this, a world-wide effort to reach many of the poorest families with micro-credit was launched. Eighteen months after the Beijing Conference on 2-4, February 1997, more than 2900 people, representing 1500 institutions from 137 countries gathered at the Micro-Credit Summit in Washington, DC. Together they set the ambitious goal of reaching 100 million of the world's poorest families, especially the women of those families with credit for self employment and other financial and business services by the year 2005.

STATEMENT OF THE PROBLEM

Integrated Rural Development Programme (IRDP) launched for poverty alleviation in India was a target-oriented programme with the focus on identifying the poorest of the poor and helping them to acquire productive assets through bank loans and subsidy from the Government. The underlying assumption was that lack of productive assets was responsible for the poor being unable to better their lot. The IRDP, however, was not as successful as was visualised.

In 1982-83, Development of Women and Children in Rural Areas (DWCRA) was launched in 50 district as a sub-scheme of IRDP. This was an attempt to involve women more intensively in economic activities. The focus of DWCRA was on economic activities for rural women to be taken up in groups. This was to enable them to overcome their inhibitions for activities they had never before undertaken, like going to the bank, buying an asset, keeping accounts, etc. Another objective of the group was to enable women to take a larger amount of loan, so that, by pooling their individual loans, they could start a viable non-farm activity. The DWCRA scheme was implemented like IRDP, through bank branches and District Rural Development Agencies (DRDA).

DWCRA too met with a limited success. The scheme as a whole failed to take off. It was seen that the economic activities, although well thought out, were not really feasible in the long run. It was observed that women were not ready to take on entrepreneurial roles; all they wanted was small loans for specific requirements, which were mainly for consumption purposes.

Despite these schemes and several others [Training of Rural Youth for Self-Employment (TRYSEM), Supply of Improved Toolkits to Rural Artisans (SITRA)], the credit and poverty problem in the rural area continues. According to the Government of India's Ministry of Rural Development, "while the antipoverty programmes have been strengthened in successive years and while in terms of percentage, poverty levels have reduced from 56.44 per cent of India's population in 1973-74 to 37.27 per cent in 1993-94, the number of rural poor has, more or less, remained static and is estimated to be about 244 million people. The rural poor are still dependent on informal sources of credit despite an impressive expansion of bank branch network. Although this dependence has come down from 83.7 per cent of the rural population in 1961 to 36 per cent in 1991, the problem still persists. It is no difficult to reckon the effect of such a large percentage of poor on the country's development. Obviously, the situation needs to be redressed quickly. It is an this context that the self-employment programmes assume significance for, they alone can provide income to the rural poor on a sustainable basis."[33]

The major problem with most schemes for poverty alleviation and channelising credit to the rural areas seems to be that they are not based on realistic assumptions and analysis of the rural credit markets. In earlier schemes, like IRDP, DWCRA, etc., the beneficiaries perceived the loan as a grant. They did not feel the responsibility of time or the mechanism for monitoring the repayment. This led to poor loan recovery and resulted in the scheme becoming non-viable.[34] In contrast, the repayment of loans in micro-credit schemes using SHGs is reported to be satisfactory from almost all places. This may be due to the face that the concept of SHG in Micro Credit Schemes is based on the theory of asymmetric information and peer monitoring.

The credit needs of the rural poor are determined in a complex socio-economic milieu where it is difficult to adopt project lending approach and where the dividing line between credit for consumption and productive purposes is blurred. Under the circumstances, a non-formal agency in the form of self-help groups of the poor could emerge as a promising partner of the formal agencies.

Dissatisfaction with the result of many formal credit programmes has stimulated searches for modalities that may provide effective financial services to rural poor particularly to women. Taking the lesson from the experiences of other developing countries like Bangladesh, Indonesia, Bolivia and Philippines where combination of formal and informal finance provides sustained and valuable services to poor, a few Non-Governmental Organisations (NGOs) in India, started experimenting the innovative scheme of Self Help Groups which are also called as Thrift and Credit Groups.

In India, over the years, various poverty alleviation programmes have been initiated by Government as well as voluntary organisations. Despite these efforts, not much difference is seen in the magnitude of poverty. Micro Credit has now emerged as a financial strategy to reach the urban and rural poor and is emerging as a movement at the global level. Over the last two decades, Micro Credit has acquired greater dimension and recognition as an instrument for meeting the credit needs of the poor for starting up their Income Generating Activities (IGA) or Micro Enterprises (ME). The institution of Self Help Groups (SHGs) has provided strength to Micro Credit System.[35]

Presiding over the Micro Credit Summit, 2001, organised by All India Women's Conference, New Delhi, Shri Yeshwant Sinha, Honourable Minister of Finance, Government of India, stressed the need for micro-credit programmes as a tool for poverty alleviation and empowerment of women.

Micro enterprises are important sources of income and employment for a significant proportion of the rural poor. In fact, this sub-sector is perceived to be an essential part of survival strategy of poor households. The relationship between micro enterprises and poverty reduction is coming up for serious consideration among the policymakers and development programme implementers.

In this context an action research on "Micro Credit Management by Women's Self Help Groups (SHGs)" was taken up to document the experiences of the SHGs in promoting micro enterprises through micro credit interventions and evaluate the impact of the programme.

OBJECTIVES OF THE STUDY

The objectives of the study were to:

- initiate Self Help Groups (SHGs) in the rural and urban areas;
- motivate the SHGs to undertake income generation activities, availing the micro credit facilities in existence; and
- study the impact of the efforts on the SHGs in quantitative and qualitative dimensions.

SOURCES OF DATA

The study is based on both primary and secondary data.

Two separate interview schedules were administered to the members and the leaders of the SHGs initiated by the investigator to get information on their profile, saving details and lending operations. The data pertaining to incremental income, assets created and employment generated were elicited through another interview schedule administered on the micro entrepreneurs both during the pre-credit and post-credit period.

The data were also collected from the secondary sources namely, the records and monthly statements maintained by the groups. Participant observation technique was also used for collecting information from the members of the SHGs.

Two specially designed score cards were developed to study the social benefits that accrued to the members of the SHGs.

TOOLS USED IN THE ANALYSIS OF DATA

For interpreting, summarising and analysing the collected data, the tools such as paired 't' test, correlation analysis, regression analysis, chi square test and ratio analysis were extensively used. Besides, percentages, means, standard deviation, co-efficient of variation, graphs and diagrams were used wherever necessary to compare the data. Analysis was also carried out to compare the findings of the urban and rural areas and the performance of micro enterprises among different categories of activity studied under different sectors.

SWOT analysis was done to assess the strengths and weaknesses of the SHGs in Micro Credit Management.

PERIOD OF THE STUDY

As the study aims at evaluating the performance of micro-credit programme in the pre and post-credit conditions, it was felt that the reference period selected should be such that it would allow sufficient time for the programme to have its full impact on the economic and social conditions of the beneficiaries. Considering this, the reference period has been fixed as 1999-2000. Thus, those respondents who obtained the assistance, either at the end of 1996-97 or at the beginning of 1997-98, had been selected and subsequently, a pilot visit to the areas revealed that the women started gaining income only in the year 1997-98. Therefore, the year 1996-97 had been considered as the base year and 1999-2000 was taken as the reference period.

SCOPE OF THE STUDY

The current study, which was basically an action research, provided an opportunity to bring an awareness among women about their situation, discrimination of rights and opportunities as a step towards gender equality. Collective awareness-building provides a sense of group identity and the power of working as a group. Collectivisation implies cohesion of the group. Cohesion enables the members of the group to perceive common interests and act collectively. It facilitates:

- Capacity building and skill development especially the ability to plan, make decision, organise, manage and carry out activities, deal with people and institutions in the world around them.
- Participation and greater control and decision-making power in the home, community and society.
- Wider scope for the NGOs to attempt group approach.
- Creation of favourable policy environment for SHGs to easily open their bank account.
- Constitution of high powered task force to make recommendations with regard to policy and regulation of the micro finance sector.

This action research helped the women to strengthen their economic activities, create positive linkages and support for access to raw materials, skill training, marketing opportunities and credit needs.

The findings and suggestions will throw light on certain broad features of the country and as such the study be of practical use in formulating better plans.

LIMITATIONS OF THE STUDY

- The data for the present study was collected through personal interview method. Since the beneficiary groups did not maintain proper accounts and most of them were uneducated, the possibility of data bias exists and hence the data collected would only be an approximation of actual facts.
- Due to time constraint, only 40 groups could be formed for the study. Their performance and functioning might not be uniform as compared to the existing groups functioning in the Coimbatore district and Karamadai Panchayat Union.

CHAPTERISATION

Chapter 1 consists of introduction, concept and evolution of SHGs, emergence of micro credit, women empowerment, statement of the problem, objectives of the study, period of the study, sources and tools used for analysis of data, the scope and the limitations of the study.

Chapter 2 describes the growth of SHGs in India.

Chapter 3 reviews the studies related to Micro Credit and Group Dynamics.

Chapter 4 presents the methodology used in the study.

Chapter 5 evaluates the performance of the SHGs initiated by the researcher.

Chapter 6 analyses the impact of micro credit on SHG members. This chapter is divided into four sections.

Section I portrays the socio-economic profile of the micro entrepreneurs.

Section II brings out the economic return from the micro enterprises undertaken by the SHG members.

Section III examines the social benefits accrued to the members in terms of group dynamics and empowerment of women.

Section IV appraises the strengths and weaknesses of the SHGs in implementing the micro credit scheme.

Chapter 7 presents the summary of the findings, bringing out the suggestions and policy implications

REFERENCES

1. *Census of India*, 20th July (2001), www.census.India.com.
2. Mishra and Purrie, 2001, *55th NSS Round*.
3. Olson, Manuor, (1971), *The Logic of Collective Action: Public Goods and the Theory of Groups*, New York: Schaken Books, p. 15.
4. Desai, Bhupat, M. and N.V. Namboodiri, (2001), *Organising and Management of Rural Financial Sector: Text, Cases and Exercises*, New Delhi: Oxford and IBH Publishing Company Pvt. Ltd., p. 52.
5. Smith, D.H. and K. Pillheimer, (1983), "Self Help Groups As Social Movement Organisations: Social Structure and Social Change", *Research in Social Movement, Conflicts and Change*, Vol. 5, No. 2, p. 35.
6. Kaladhar, K., (1997), "Micro Finance in India: Design, Structure and Governance", *Economic and Political Weekly*, Vol. 32, No. 42, October 18, p. 21.
7. Desai, B.M. and J.W. Mellor, (1993), "Institutional Finance for Agriculture Development: An Analytical Survey of Critical Issues", *Food Policy Review 1*, U.S.A.: Washington D.C., International Food Policy Research Institute, p. 18.
8. Nanda, Y.C., (2000), *"Role of Banks in Rural Development in the New Millennium"*, Mumbai: National Bank for Agriculture and Rural Development, p. 12.
9. Srinivasan, Girija, (1997), *Training Programme on Credit and Micro Enterprise Development for the NGOs and Officials of IMY*, Lucknow: Bankers Institute for Rural Development (BIRD), pp. 18-19.
10. Gupta, R.C., (1993), *Guidelines for Field Workers on Management of Self Help Savings and Credit Groups*, New Delhi: Friedrich Ebert Stiffung, p. 3.

11. Rashtriya Mahila Kosh, (1995), *Annual Report*, Printed at New Delhi: Veerendra Printers, p. 11.

12. Satis, P. and P. Das, (1997), *Linkage of SHGs with Formal Financial Agencies Experience of Other Countries in Asia*, Working Paper 4, Lucknow: Bankers Institute of Rural Development, p. 2.

13. Shivakumar, L., (1995), Self Help Groups, *Social Welfare*, Oct. 6, Vol. XI, No. 6, pp. 8-10.

14. Dwaraki and Kumarasan, B., (1997), Self Help Groups—Quo Vaids? *Social Welfare*, June, 1997, Vol. 44, No. 3, p. 40.

15. Murugan, K.R. and Dharmalingam, (2000), Self Help Groups—New Women's Movement in Tamil Nadu, *J. Social Welfare*, 47 (45), pp. 9-12.

16. Bouman, F.J.A. (1984), "Informal Savings and Credit Arrangements in Developing Countries: Observations from Sri Lanka" in Dale W. Adams, G.H. Graham and J.D. Von Pischke (eds.), *Undermining Rural Development with Cheap Credit*, London: Westview Press, pp. 40-42.

17. Desai, Bhupat, M. and N.V. Namboodiri, (1996), "Whither Rural Financial Institutions", *Economic and Political Weekly*, August 3, Vol. 31, No. 31, p. 10.

18. Zeller, Manfred and Manohar Sharma, (1988), Rural Finance and Poverty Alleviation, *Food Policy Report*, U.S.A.: Washington, D.C., International Food Policy Research Institute, p. 6.

19. United Nations, (1998), "United Nations General Assemble Resolution 52/194 Passed in December, 1997 (1998)", in Count Down 2005, *Newsletter of the Micro Credit Summit Campaign*, Vol. 1, No. 3, February/March, p. 21.

20. Swarup, V., (2001), "Micro Finance Could Become a Macro Mess", *The Economic Times*, February 26, (Ahmedabad), p. 7.

21. Kaladhar, K., (1997), "Micro Finance in India: Design, Structure and Governance", *Economic and Political Weekly*, Vol. 32, No. 42, October 18, p. 5.

22. World Bank, (1997), "Introducing Savings in Micro Credit Institutions: When and How?", *CGAP Focus Note*, U.S.A.: Washington, D.C., Consultative Group to Assist the Poorest of the Poor, p. 25.

23. Edwards, John, H.Y., (1989), "Rotating Credit/Associations and Lotteries as Financial Instruments for the Poor", Tulane University, Economics Department, New Orleans, La Processed.

24. Hossain, Mahabub, (1998), Credit for Alleviation of Rural Poverty: The Grameen Bank in Bangladesh, *Research Report No. 65*, Washington, D.C.: International Food Policy Research Institute, Processed.

25. National Bank for Agriculture and Rural Development (NABARD), (1999), Mumbai: *Report of the Task Force on Supportive Policy and Regulatory Framework for Micro Finance.*

26. Small Industries Development Bank of India (SIDBI) (1998), *Annual Report*, New Delhi.

27. Department of Women and Child Development, (1996), *Annual Report Part-IV*, Ministry of Human Resources Development, Government of India, pp. 49-51 and 93.

28. *Hindustan Times*, 2001, July 13, p. 9.

29. United Nations, (1996), Fourth World Conference on Women, *The Beijings Declaration and the Platform for Action*, Chennai, New York: Department of Public Information, pp. 25-39.

30. Devadas, R.P., (1986), Management of Development Programmes for Women and Children through Home Science, Vol. 5, Coimbatore: Sri Avinashilingam Trust Institutions, pp. 225-227.

31. International Labour Organisation (ILO), (1984), "Women's Participation in Economic Activity", Geneva: *World Employment Programme Research Working Paper No. 42*, p. 17.

32. Sinha Archana, (2002), "Types of SHGs and Their Work", *Social Welfare Issue*, February, p. 16.

33. Government of India, (1999), *Swarnjayanti Gram Swarozgar Yojana: Guidelines*, New Delhi: Ministry of Rural Development, p. 10.

34. Rath, N., (1985), "Garibi Hatao: Can IRDP Do It? "*Economic and Political Weekly*, Vol. 20, No. 6, February 9, pp. 238-246.

    Rao Dinkar, K. V.A. Deshpande and A. Dharmadhikari, (1990), Development of Women and Children in Rural Areas (DWCRA), Velhe, District, Pune, An Action Research Project sponsored by UNICEF India, Pune: National Institute of Bank Management.

35. Joshi, S.C. (2002), "Micro Credit Not Charity", *Social Welfare Issue*, February, pp. 12-14.

2

Growth of Self Help Groups in India

Introduction

The ability of the formal banking sector to serve the needs of the poor rural clientele is quite apparent. Institutional credit has not penetrated to the lower income groups. The thrust of the organised sectors, within the priority sector lending framework, has been on productive activities, whereas the poor, the large majority of whom are landless, need credit mainly for financing income—consumption gap or tiding over occasional crisis and emergencies. Obviously, the need, terms and modes of delivery do not match. This could well be the reasons for the increased dependence of rural people, more markedly of the poor women, on informal credit sources like moneylenders, contractors, traders and intermediaries.

In this context, to bridge the gap between the demand and supply of funds in the lower rungs of rural society, Self Help Groups (SHGs), which operate on the principles of Self Help, mutual trust and co-operation have emerged as informal financial institutions for the poor under the guidance and support of Non-Government Organisations (NGOs).

The concept that SHGs could work as local financial intermediaries eventually gained wide recognition when NABARD began exploring the possibilities of establishing linkage between SHGs and banks. The Bank-SHG linkage scheme mounted at a time when there was widespread rethinking about antipoverty policies focussing on participation of the poor in income generating activities. The paradigm of development, which emerged out of these experiments has its roots in self-reliance, self-sufficiency and self-help.

The Honourable Union Finance Minister in his budget speech for the year 2000-2001, announced the certain of a Micro Finance Development Fund in NABARD with a start-up contribution of Rs. 1,000 million from Reserve Bank of India, NABARD, banks and others. NABARD has already contributed Rs. 400 million out of its resources and created the fund. NABARD has been functioning as a catalyst in providing the necessary impetus for accelerating the growth of the SHG-linkage with the policy support from the Government of India and Reserve Bank of India.

SHG-BANK LINKAGE PROGRAMME

It is significant that SHG-bank linkage programme gathered momentum in the country and credit linkage during 1999-2000 was more than twice the cumulative performance of bank in credit-linking of SHGs as an 31st March 1999. The number of SHGs credit-linked for the years 1997-98 to 1999-2000 are depicted in Figure 2.1.

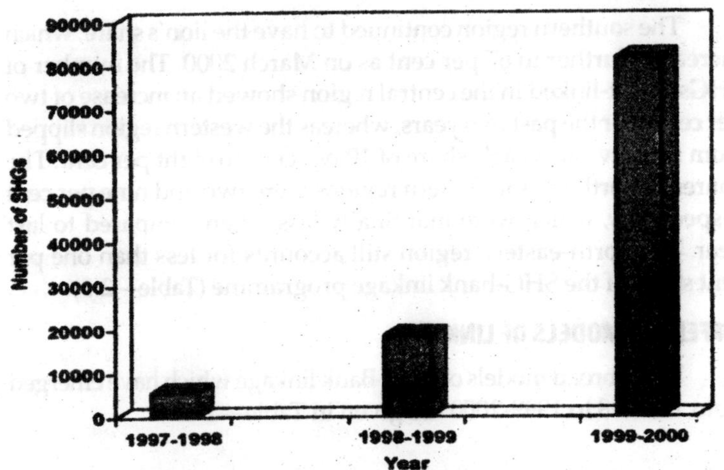

Source: NABARD and Micro Finance (1999-2000)

Fig. 2.1: Number of SHGs Credit-Linked during the years 1997-98 to 1999-2000

The significant success of the programme was due to the active involvement of over 700 NGOs, 7,500 branches of 266 banks, policy support from Government of India and Reserve Bank of India, increased participation from the state governments, as also the development policy initiatives and capacity building of partner agencies by NABARD. SHG-bank linkage programme covered 362 districts in 24 states and union territories of the country.

STATE-WISE OUTREACH

The state of Andhra Pradesh accounted for the largest number of SHGs credit linked during 1999-2000 (29,242), followed by Uttar Pradesh (7,744), Tamil Nadu (7,671) and Karnataka (3,167). Some of the states which recorded significant increases in SHG promotion and credit linking during 1999-2000 were Maharashtra (3,029), West Bengal (2,465) and Orissa (2,050). The region-wise/state-wise performance during the year 1997-98 to 1999-2000 is presented in Table—2.1. Details of the cumulative physical and financial progress as on 31st March 2000 are presented in Table—2.2.

Regional Spread

The southern region continued to have the lion's share, which increased further to 67 per cent as on March 2000. The number of SHGs credit-linked in the central region showed an increase of two per cent over the past two years, whereas the western region slipped from its previous year's share of 10 per cent to eight per cent. The shares of northern and eastern regions were two and nine per cent respectively, which were marginally less when compared to last year. The north-eastern region still accounts for less than one per cent share of the SHG-bank linkage programme (Table—2.3).

DIFFERENT MODELS OF LINKAGE

Three broad models of SHG-Bank linkage which have emerged from 1997-98 to 1999-2000 are given in Table—2.4.

Table—2.1 Region/State-wise performance during the years 1997-1998 to 1999-2000

(Rs. in million)

S. No.	Region/State	1997-1998			1998-1999			1999-2000		
		No. of SHGs Linked	*Bank Loan*	*Refinance*	*No. of SHGs Linked*	*Bank Loan*	*Refinance*	*No. of SHGs Linked*	*Bank Loan*	*Refinance*
1	*2*	*3*	*4*	*5*	*6*	*7*	*8*	*9*	*10*	*11*
A.	**Northern Region**									
1.	Himachal Pradesh	71	0.45	0.44	133	1.44	1.61	48	8.72	1.00
2.	Rajasthan	68	4.03	1.49	465	11.66	4.39	526	25.62	13.00
3.	Haryana	3	0.06	0.07	4	0.49	0.44	107	5.82	3.00
4.	Punjab				1	0.04		18	0.98	0.30
5.	Jammu & Kashmir				2	0.02	0.02	53	0.53	0.10
	Total (A)	**142**	**4.54**	**2.00**	**605**	**13.65**	**6.46**	**752**	**41.67**	**17.40**
B.	**North Eastern Region**									
6.	Assam				10	0.21	0.02	46	0.47	0.40
7.	Meghalaya	5	0.14	0.13	30	0.79	0.52	49	0.78	0.10
8.	Tripura				3	0.13	0.05	1	0.06	0.00
9.	Sikkim				1	0.01	0.01		0.00	0.00
10.	Manipur				5	0.20	0.10		0.00	0.00
	Total (B)	**5**	**0.14**	**0.13**	**49**	**1.34**	**0.70**	**96**	**1.30**	**0.50**

(Table Contd...)

1	2	3	4	5	6	7	8	9	10	11
C.	**Eastern Region**									
11.	Orissa	290	2.33	2.33	975	9.22	9.18	2021	18.09	17.80
12.	Bihar	119	1.03	0.56	121	1.80	1.80	857	12.49	10.40
13.	West Bengal	232	1.52	1.63	554	4.15	4.11	2317	18.55	16.90
14.	UT of A & N Islands	7	0.09	0.09	3	0.28	0.25	9	0.23	0.20
	Total (C)	**648**	**4.97**	**4.61**	**1653**	**15.45**	**15.34**	**5204**	**49.36**	**45.30**
D.	**Central Region**									
15.	Madhya Pradesh	169	5.73	2.30	461	6.08	2.16	1533	25.84	22.40
16.	Uttar Pradesh	389	6.72	6.01	1464	11.99	11.63	7744	68.72	20.90
	Total (D)	**558**	**12.45**	**8.31**	**1925**	**18.07**	**13.79**	**9277**	**94.55**	**43.30**
E.	**Western Region**									
17.	Gujarat	467	4.09	2.57	879	13.46	12.81	1345	21.28	18.80
18.	Maharashtra	448	7.80	7.24	1058	22.41	22.15	3029	55.09	13.50
19.	Goa	1	0.04		4	0.09	0.12	14	0.80	0.80
	Total (E)	**916**	**11.93**	**9.81**	**1941**	**35.96**	**35.08**	**4388**	**77.17**	**33.10**

(Table Contd...)

1	2	3	4	5	6	7	8	9	10	11
F.	**Southern Region**									
20.	Andhra Pradesh	1322	31.75	31.64	6579	127.26	127.21	29242	682.56	548.90
21.	Karnataka	1148	23.02	22.81	2002	42.99	42.23	3167	118.37	65.80
22.	Kerala	536	8.61	6.24	1291	22.47	10.04	1709	56.55	29.20
23.	Tamil Nadu	442	21.79	21.71	2618	55.75	55.75	7671	27.31	186.80
24.	UT of Pondicherry	2	0.02	0.02	15	0.14	0.14	144	10.27	10.40
	Total (F)	**3450**	**85.20**	**82.42**	**12505**	**248.61**	**235.37**	**41933**	**1095.05**	**841.10**
	Grand Total	**5719**	**119.23**	**107.29**	**18678**	**333.01**	**306.74**	**61650**	**1359.11**	**980.70**

Source: NABARD, 2000.

Table—2.2 SHG-Bank linkage programme—regional spread of physical and financial progress cumulatively as at March 2000

(Rs. in Million)

S. No.	Region/State	Cumulative No. of SHGs credit linked	Cumulative No. of SHGs refinance linked		Cumulative bank loans	Cumulative NABARD refinance
			Total	Of which women		
1	2	3	4	5	6	7
A.	**Northern Region**					
	Himachal Pradesh	983	402	402	12.22	3.86
	Rajasthan	1941	1236	930	45.57	22.66
	Haryana	203	121	6	6.57	3.57
	Punjab	40	20	2	1.05	0.30
	Jammu & Kashmir	55	55	55	0.55	0.12
	Total (A)	**3222**	**1834**	**1395**	**65.96**	**30.51**
B.	**North Eastern Region**					
	Assam	67	60	54	0.67	0.42
	Meghalaya	118	118	4	2.89	1.92
	Tripura	5	5	3	0.32	0.05
	Sikkim	1	1	1	0.01	0.01
	Manipur	5	5	5	0.20	0.10
	Total (B)	**196**	**189**	**67**	**4.09**	**2.50**

(Table Contd...)

1	2	3	4	5	6	7
C.	**Eastern Region**					
	Orissa	4068	4039	3480	34.39	34.04
	Bihar	1910	1353	1332	17.88	14.41
	West Bengal .	3397	3249	2784	25.79	23.01
	UT of A & N Island	23	23	11	0.66	0.59
	Total (C)	**9398**	**8664**	**7607**	**78.72**	**72.05**
D.	**Central Region**					
	Madhya Pradesh	2303	2266	2013	41.02	27.46
	Uttar Pradesh	12953	10556	4525	92.22	41.31
	Total (D)	**15256**	**12822**	**6538**	**133.24**	**68.77**
E.	**Western Region**					
	Gujarat	3005	2843	2420	42.05	37.40
	Maharashtra	4959	4959	4470	92.99	49.51
	Goa	19	19	19	0.93	0.92
	Total (E)	**7983**	**7821**	**6909**	**135.97**	**87.83**

(Table Contd...)

1	2	3	4	5	6	7
F.	**Southern Region**					
	Andhra Pradesh	48507	37966	37843	865.81	731.79
	Karnataka	10610	8759	4510	223.01	169.46
	Kerala	5551	4826	4701	95.54	51.47
	Tamil Nadu	13884	11596	10785	316.97	276.24
	UT of Pondicherry	168	168	166	10.51	10.64
	Total (F)	**78720**	**63315**	**58005**	**1511.84**	**1239.60**
	Grand Total	**114775**	**94645**	**80521**	**1929.82**	**1501.26**

Source: NABARD, 2000.

Table—2.3 Region-wise spread of the SHG—Bank linkage programme during the years 1997-98 to 1999-2000

Region	*% share in linkage (Cumulative) as on*		
	March 1998	*March 1999*	*March 2000*
Northern	3	3	2
North-eastern	< 1	< 1	< 1
Western	10	10	8
Eastern	13	10	9
Central	11	11	13
Southern	62	65	67
Total	**100**	**100**	**100**

Source: NABARD, 2000.

Table—2.4 SHG-Bank linkage programme model-wise position cumulatively

(Figure in percentage)

Model	*1997-1998*	*1998-1999*	*1999-2000*
I	13	17	14
II	45	56	70
III	42	27	16

Source: NABARD, 2000.

Model I: Bank—SHG—Members

In this model, the bank itself acts as a Self Help Group Promoting Institution (SHPI). It takes initiatives in forming the groups, nurturing them over a period of time, opening their savings accounts and then providing credit to them after satisfying itself about their maturity to absorb credit. This model formed 14 per cent of the cumulative number of SHGs credit-linked up to 31st March 2000, as against 17 per cent in the year 1999. Although the percentage share shows reduction, more and more branches, especially of the RRBs, are getting involved in this mode.

Model II: Bank-(Facilitating Agency)—SHG—Members

In this model, groups are formed by facilitating agencies like NGOs, government agencies, or other community-based organisations. The groups are nurtured and trained by these agencies. The share of SHGs financed under this model has significantly increased to 70 per cent during 1999-2000, as against 56 per cent last year. The increase is attributed to the participation of a large number of NGOs, as also the wider involvement of state governments through their development agencies like the DRDA, DWDA and some of the centrally sponsored social sector missions.

Model III: Bank—NGO—MFI—SHG—Members

Due to various reasons, banks in some areas are sometimes not in a position to even finance SHGs promoted and nurtured by other agencies. In such cases, the NGOs act as both facilitators and Micro Finance Intermediaries (MFIs).

Under this model, the NGOs act as both facilitators and Micro Finance Intermediaries (MFIs). The share of cumulative number of SHGs supported under this model declined to 16 per cent, as against 27 per cent in the year 1998-1999. However, this model is likely to be found more conveniently by banks for credit linkage in the coming years, when very large number of SHGs would be required to be linked by small sized branches of banks.

Among the three models, the second one namely direct linkage with NGO acting as facilitator is found to be popular. The SHG linkage programme of various models as on 31st March, 2000 is presented vide Table—2.5.

Table—2.5 Different models of SHG—Bank linkage programme as on 31st March 2000 (Cumulative)

	SHGs		*Bank Loan*		*Refinance*	
Model	*No*	*%*	*Amount*	*%*	*Amount*	*%*
I	13,561	14	339.79	18	228.15	15
II	65,636	70	1,339.95	69	1,087.31	73
III	15,448	16	250.10	13	185.80	12
Total	**94,645**	**100**	**1,929.82**	**100**	**1,501.26**	**100**

Source: Micro Credit Innovation, Department, NABARD, 2000.

Out of 94,645 groups under the linkage scheme in 2000, 13,561 groups were directly linked to SHG without any intervention by NGO, 65,636 groups had been linked to bank with NGO acting as facilitator and 15,448 groups were linked to banks indirectly where NGOs act as on lending intermediaries.

SHG LINKAGE PROGRAMME UNDER PRIORITY SECTOR LENDING

According to the recommendations made by the working group, under the Chairmanship of Shri S.K. Kalia, in 1996 SHG programme has been made into a regular programme under the priority sector lending of banks. The working group expressed the view that the linkage of SHG with banks was a cost-effective, transparent and flexible approach to improve the accessibility of credit from the formal banking system to the unreached poor. The poor recommended that:

1. The banks should treat the linkage programme as a business opportunity for reaching the rural poor and make it a part of their corporate strategy;
2. The programme be made a part of service area approach and Lead Bank reporting system;
3. This concept be made a part of the regular training curriculum of banks;
4. Lending of banks to SHGs be made a separate segment under the priority sector; and
5. Review and monitoring of SHGs linkage programme should be carried out periodically.

The SHG linkage programme bank-wise position is presented vide Table—2.6.

Table—2.6 Distribution of SHGs as on 31st March 2000 agency-wise (Cumulative)

(Rs. in million)

Agency	*No. of SHGs*	*% to total*	*Bank loan*	*% to total*	*Refinance*	*% to total*
Commercial Banks	51619	55	1278.33	66	934.04	62
RRBs	38998	41	574.59	30	513.81	34
Co-operatives	4028	4	76.90	4	53.41	4
Total	**94645**	**100**	**1929.82**	**100**	**1501.26**	**100**

Source: Micro finance and NABARD report 1999-2000.

A total of 266 banks participated in the SHG credit linking programme during the year 1999-2000. These comprised 40 commercial banks (CBs), 165 RRBs and 61 co-operatives. The share of commercial banks in the aggregate number of SHGs credit linked continued to remain at the highest level with 55 per cent followed by RRBs (41 per cent) and co-operatives (four per cent) from a level of about 34 per cent to 41 per cent, while the share of co-operatives has remained almost stagnant.

The state-wise and bank-wise number of SHGs linked to commercial banks is presented in Table—2.7 A and B.

Besides participation by all the 27 public sector commercial banks, 13 private sector banks also participated in the programme. During the year, with NABARD refinance, State Bank of India has credit-linked the highest number SHGs (10,472), followed by Andhra Bank (6,169) and State Bank of Hyderabad (4,681). The other Banks having a significant share in the programme were Canara Bank, Indian Bank, Bank of Baroda, Indian Overseas Bank and Syndicate Bank. Among the private sector Banks, Vasya Bank has linked the maximum SHGs followed by Bank of Madura, Karnataka Bank, Global Trust Bank and South Indian Bank.

Table—2.7 A SHG-Bank linkage programme state-wise cumulative number of SHGs linked with Commercial Banks (As at 31st March 2000)

(Number of SHGs)

S. No.	Banks	A.P.	Bihar	Gujarat	Goa	H.P.	Haryana	J & K	Karnataka	Kerala	M.P.	Maharashtra
1	2	3	4	5	6	7	8	9	10	11	12	13
I.	**Commercial Banks**											
A.	**Public Sector Banks**											
1.	Allahabad Bank	32	30									
2.	Andhra Bank	6169										
3.	Bank of Baroda	1111	10	941	2				31	15	20	7
4.	Bank of India	261	141	26	5		6		3	69	197	376
5.	Bank of Maharashtra	25							3		52	578
6.	Canara Bank	1356	71		4		1		465	421		14
7.	Corporation Bank	676			2				191	91		
8.	Central Bank of India	414	3	30		12			9	3	8	146
9.	Dena Bank	31		418							11	9
10.	Indian Bank	1249		18			1		2	125		44

(Table Contd...)

1	2	3	4	5	6	7	8	9	10	11	12	13
11.	Indian Overseas Bank	640		6	1				13	134		
12.	Oriental Bank of Commerce											
13.	Punjab & Sind Bank					3						
14.	Punjab National Bank	3	1	8		62	7		4		1	
15.	State Bank of India	4600	146	305	2	65	7	43	1015	135	68	495
16.	State Bank of Bikaner & Jaipur											
17.	State Bank of Hyderabad	4588							2			91
18.	State Bank of Indore										288	
19.	State Bank of Mysore	27							238			
20.	State Bank of Patiala					20						
21.	State Bank of Saurashtra			39								
22.	State Bank of Travancore									1071		
23.	Syndicate Bank	1139							432	284		
24.	Union Bank of India	796		33	2	2				188		13
25.	United Bank of India											
26.	UCO Bank	47	18		1	93				2		
27.	Vijaya Bank	290							829	5		
	Total 'A'	**23454**	**420**	**1824**	**19**	**257**	**22**	**43**	**3237**	**2543**	**645**	**1773**

(Table Contd...)

1	2	3	4	5	6	7	8	9	10	11	12	13
B.	**Private Sector Banks**											
1.	Bank of Madura Ltd.											
2.	Bank of Rajasthan Ltd.											
3.	Global Trust Bank Ltd.	263										
4.	Jammu & Kashmir Bank Ltd.							7				
5.	Karnataka Bank Ltd.								393			
6.	South Indian Bank Ltd.	121								85		
7.	Tamilnadu Mercantile Bank Ltd.											
8.	Vysya Bank Ltd.	613							160			
9.	Catholic Syrian Bank Ltd.									12		
10.	Federal Bank Ltd.									30		
11.	Lord Krishna Bank Ltd.									12		
12.	City Union Bank Ltd.											
13.	Laxmi Vilas Bank Ltd.											
	Total 'B'	**997**						**7**	**553**	**139**		
	Grand Total 'A' + 'B'	**24451**	**420**	**1824**	**19**	**257**	**22**	**50**	**3790**	**2682**	**645**	**3611**

(Table Contd...)

S. No.	Banks	Punjab	Orissa	Rajasthan	Tamil Nadu	U.P.	W.B.	U.T. (P)	Sikkim	Maniur	Meghalaya	Maharashtra	Total
1	2	3	4	5	6	7	8	9	10	11	12	13	14
I.	**Commercial Banks**												
A.	**Public Sector Banks**												
1.	Allahabad Bank			2	23	29	146						262
2.	Andhra Bank												6169
3.	Bank of Baroda		115	139	43	104	9	3					2550
4.	Bank of India		180		365	153	27						1809
5.	Bank of Maharashtra												658
6.	Canara Bank		308		1052	149						4	3845
7.	Corporation Bank				176								1136
8.	Central Bank of India		36	1	208	170			1				1041
9.	Dena Bank				1								470
10.	Indian Bank		15		1536	2	6	27					3025
11.	Indian Overseas Bank	5	118		1282		3						2202
12.	Oriental Bank of Commerce			117		876							993
13.	Punjab & Sind Bank					4							7
14.	Punjab National Bank		5	45	77	33							246

(*Table Contd...*)

1	2	3	4	5	6	7	8	9	10	11	12	13	14
15.	State Bank of India		533	12	2579	186	256	16		5	1	3	10472
16.	State Bank of Bikaner & Jaipur			69									69
17.	State Bank of Hyderabad												4681
18.	State Bank of Indore												288
19.	State Bank of Mysore			1									266
20.	State Bank of Patiala												20
21.	State Bank of Saurashtra												39
22.	State Bank of Travancore				14								1085
23.	Syndicate Bank		42		166	14							2077
24.	Union Bank of India		26	2	406	81		120					1669
25.	United Bank of India		1				606						607
26.	UCO Bank	1	41	14	17		232	2				7	475
27.	Vijaya Bank			3	13								1140
	Total 'A'	**6**	**1420**	**404**	**7959**	**1801**	**1285**	**168**	**1**	**5**	**1**	**14**	**47301**
B.	**Private Sector Banks**												
1.	Bank of Madura Ltd.				441								441
2.	Bank of Rajasthan Ltd.			41									41
3.	Global Trust Bank Ltd.												263
4.	Jammu & Kashmir Bank Ltd.												7

(Table Contd...)

1	2	3	4	5	6	7	8	9	10	11	12	13	14
5.	Karnataka Bank Ltd.												393
6.	South Indian Bank Ltd.												206
7.	Tamilnadu Mercantile Bank Ltd.				20								20
8.	Vysya Bank Ltd.												773
9.	Catholic Syrian Bank Ltd.												12
10.	Federal Bank Ltd.												30
11.	Lord Krishna Bank Ltd.												12
12.	City Union Bank Ltd.				49								49
13.	Laxmi Vilas Bank Ltd.				22								22
	Total 'B'			**41**	**532**								**2269**
	Grand Total 'A' + 'B'	**6**	**1420**	**656**	**8491**	**1801**	**1285**	**168**	**1**	**5**	**1**	**14**	**51619**

Source: NABARD, 2000.

Bank-wise details of SHG-Bank linkage programme in Tamil Nadu as on 31st March 2000 is given in Table—2.8.

Table—2.8 Banks involved in SHG linkage scheme in Tamil Nadu

S. No.	Bank	Number of SHGs
1.	Allahabad Bank	23
2.	Bank of Baroda	43
3.	Bank of India	365
4.	Canara Bank	1052
5.	Central Bank of India	208
6.	Corporation Bank	176
7.	Dena Bank	1
8.	Indian Bank	1536
9.	Indian Overseas Bank	1282
10.	Punjab National Bank	77
11.	State Bank of India	2579
12.	State Bank of Travencore	14
13.	Syndicate Bank	166
14.	Union Bank of India	406
15.	UCO Bank	17
16.	Vijaya Bank	13
17.	Bank of Madura Ltd.	441
18.	Tamilnadu Mercantile Bank Ltd.	20
19.	City Union Bank Ltd.	49
20.	Laxi Vilas Bank Ltd.	22
21.	Adhiyamman GB	330
22.	Pandiyan GB	2177
23.	Vallalar GB	431
24.	Dharmapuri CCB	160
25.	Tirvarur CCB	7
	Total	**11596**

Source: Micro Finance and NABARD, 1999-2000.

In Tamil Nadu, out of the total 11,596 groups, 73.2 per cent of the groups are promoted by commercial banks, 25.3 per cent of the groups are promoted by Regional Rural Banks and 1.5 per cent of the groups are promoted by co-operatives. Among the 20 commercial banks involved in the scheme, the performance of State Bank of India is commendable, followed by Indian Bank and Indian Overseas Bank.

PARTICIPATING NON-GOVERNMENTAL ORGANISATION

As against 550 NGOs during 1998-1999, the number of NGOs which participated in credit linking SHGs during 1999-2000 rose to 718. These NGOs participated in the linkage programme either as facilitators or as financial intermediaries. As on 31st March 2000, 70 per cent of the SHGs were linked through NGOs and other agencies acting only as facilitators and another 16 per cent through the financial intermediation of NGOs (*Source*— Micro Finance and NABARD, Report 1999-2000).

GOVERNMENT EFFORTS IN PROMOTING SHGs FOR WOMEN

In the Ninth Plan a special thrust was given on expeditious adoption of the National Policy for empowerment of women and towards raising their status. Over the decades of planned development the changed emphasis of women's programmes from purely welfare and consumption-oriented approach to a more pragmatic and development-oriented one, has recognised women as productive workers and contributors to the economy of the country, to some extent, in the upper social and economic strata of the society.

The National Commission on Self Employment of Women focussed on the tremendous contribution that the women of different sectors made to the national economy which led to specific programmes like STEP (Support to Training for Employment Programme), DWACRA (Development of Women and Children in Rural Areas), RMK (Rashtriya Mahila Kosh) etc. Women's development corporations set up in different states are also making concerted efforts towards improving the condition of women by upgrading their skills through training programmes and offering greater employment opportunities to them through schemes like public distribution, dairy development, food preservation, social forestry, rural marketing, etc., which are related to them in traditional occupations like agriculture, animal husbandry, fishery and others. However, prioritising to agriculture and rural development, generating productive employment and eradication of poverty, ensuring food and nutritional security for the women and children are some of the objectives of the common minimum needs programme of the government which would definitely result in the development and empowerment of women.

RASHTRIYA MAHILA KOSH

The Government of India sponsored Rashtriya Mahila Kosh (RMK) was constituted as a registered society on 30th March, 1993. The main objective of RMK is to facilitate credit support or micro finance to poor women for income generating activities. RMK mainly uses NGOs as its channelising agencies for identification of borrowers, delivery of credit support and recovery. Since its inception, upto January 31, 1999, RMK has been able to sanction credit limits of Rs. 57.09 crore through 367 NGOs to benefit 2,77,662 women. In addition, RMK has also supported the formation of women's thrift and credit societies particularly known as SHGs through its partner NGOs. RMK also offers support to develop and stabilise SHGs and to conduct awareness programmes among rural and urban women.

INDIRA MAHILA YOJANA

Indira Mahila Yojana was launched on 20th August, 1995. IMY is a centrally sponsored scheme, a strategy to empower women by ensuring them direct access to resources through a sustained process of mobilisation and convergence of all the ongoing sectoral programmes. Under IMY, a very strong emphasis was laid on the formation of women's SHGs at grassroot level under the Indira Mahila Kendras. IMY scheme is operated at the district level as a subplan to percolate to the village level appropriately through Indira Mahila Block Society (IMBS) at the block level and Indira Mahila Kendra (IMK) at the village level. IMBs and IMKs are established as registered societies and supported by mechanisms, both at the state and central levels. IMY has so far been adopted in 200 blocks of the country.

On 13 July, 2001, the Department of Women and Child Development announced the launching of "Swayamsidhha" an integrated self help group based programme to empower women by amalgamating the Indira Mahila Yojana and Mahila Samridhi Yojana. The scheme is aimed towards holistic empowerment of women through awareness generation and economic empowerment (*Hindustan Times*, 2001). The Annual Report (2000-2001) of the Department indicates that by the end of January 2001, nearly 5,460 SHGs were formed by 85 village officers in different states as against the targeted number of 2850. It is estimated that a total of 12,000 SHGs exist as a means of empowering rural women.

SHGs FORMED BY THE GOVERNMENT DEPARTMENT IN TAMIL NADU

The International Fund for Agriculture Development (IFAD) assisted Tamil Nadu Women's Development Project was first introduced in Dharmapuri district in November 1989. It was extended to Villupuram, Cuddalore and Salem districts during 1991-1992 and then to Madurai, Theni and Ramanathapuram districts during 1993-1994. The Tamil Nadu Corporation for Development of Women Ltd. was the implementing agency and Indian Bank was the nodal bank for the project. Under the scheme, Rs. 48.16 crore were disbursed as credit and Rs. 32.33 crore as subsidy totaling Rs. 80.49 crore to 87541 SHG members with an average repayment of 85 per cent. About 5207 SHGs with 120960 women members accumulated a total saving corpus of Rs. 22.89 crore under the IFAD scheme which came to a close on 31st December 1998. The ultimate objective of IFAD was to leave behind self reliant and sustainable SHGs through a process of careful and slow withdrawal by NGOs and TNCDW in a phased manner. Sustainability of the groups was measured by the following parameters.

— Formulation of long term mission by the SHGs

— Repayment of loan at more than 90 per cent

— High group grading

— Non-dependence on NGOs and TNCDW

— Ability to manage their own affairs

— Adoption of best and healthy practices in family and SHG

— Perceptible improvement in the income of the members

— Networking-SHG participation in federations

— Contribution to social development

— High degree of cohesion between group members

Mahalir Thittam Project

In the light of the experiences gained in the implementation of the IFAD assisted TNWDP since 1989-1990, the Mahalir Thittam has been launched with state funds to cover the entire state in a phased manner. It was an ambitious five year project envisaging the formation of 60,000 SHGs comprising 10 lakh women below the poverty line in the state by the terminating year of the project, with a total financial outlay of Rs. 1,440 crore.

The mission of Mahalir Thittam is to:

- build the capacity of the poor and disadvantaged women to enable them cross all social and economic barriers and thereby facilitating their full development;
- achieve the equality of status of poor women as participants, decision-makers and beneficiaries in the economic, social, cultural and democratic spheres of life;
- create or reorient democratic, economic and social processes and institutions to enable poor women to participate fully and actively in decision-making in the family and community and at the local, district, state and national levels;
- encourage women to work together with men as equal partners and to inspire a new generation of women and men to work together for equality, sustainable development and communal harmony;
- promote and ensure the human rights of women at all stages of their life-cycles; and
- advocate changes in government policies and programmes in favour of disadvantaged women.

District-wise performance report of Mahalir Thittam as on 31st December, 1999 was given vide Table—2.9.

Table—2.9 Progress of SHGs under mahalir Thittam as on 31.12.1999

District	Women population	Number of SHGs to be formed	Number of SHGs formed	Group savings (Rs. in lakhs)	*SHGs assisted with NABARD credit* Number of SHGs	Amount (lakh)
Dharmapuri	117800	3000	1752	618.27	249	129.04
Salem	94200	2220	1040	329.09	70	12.85
Villupuram	119950	3000	1896	534.20	32	10.19
Madurai	84650	2000	1118	295.94	17	5.31
Ramnad	57500	1850	1459	331.21	51	13.07
Namakkal	94200	2220	1647	83.39	37	6.55
Cuddalore	119950	2820	1502	96.32	109	12.19
Theni	84650	1100	540	40.33	–	–
Thiruvallur	113950	2680	1065	86.67	42	9.69
Vellore	149600	3520	1404	61.12	16	2.00
Thiruvarur	75266	1770	1464	70.29	107	14.28
Karur	68400	1610	1031	43.96	314	57.13
Virudunagar	78000	1830	659	61.99	61	9.53
Thuthukudi	74600	1750	705	70.29	129	21.94
Trichy	68400	1610	492	29.22	51	7.75
Tiruvanamalai	101300	3000	409	16.11	38	4.47
Pudukottai	66500	1610	413	13.29	–	–
Tirunelveli	127200	3000	644	28.59	8	2.50
Sivagangai	54800	1900	623	26.19	5	0.77
Erode	113500	2670	243	14.55	6	2.10
Nilgiris	35200	900	331	16.55	–	–
Coimbatore*	171100	2000	100	3.17	–	–
Dindigul*	87000	2050	–	–	–	–
Kancheepuram*	113950	2680	280	1.17	–	–
Nagapatnam*	75266	2250	–	–	–	–
Perambalur*	68400	1610	–	–	–	–
Tanjavur*	75266	1900	–	–	–	–
Kanyakumari*	59700	1400	–	–	–	–
Total	**2550298**	**60000**	**20817**	**2861.37**	**1342**	**321.36**

* Project offices in these 7 districts were opened only on 01.11.1999 and work has just commenced.

Source: Tamil Nadu Corporation for Development of Women Ltd.

DANIDA—TANWA Groups

DANIDA (Danish International Development Agency) assisted TANWA (Tamil Nadu Women in Agriculture) project, has been in operation in Tamil Nadu since 1986. The objective of this project is to acquaint small and marginal women farmers with technological skills in agriculture through Training-cum-Extension programme. RASEE (Rural Action for Self Employment and Education) formed in February, 1996 by a few members of the Resource Group of Phase I of the project is now engaged in promoting TANWA farm women groups on the lives of NABARD SHG concept. About 135 groups are functioning in various districts of the state. NABARD has been extending faculty/financial support for the training programmes organised for the project officers of the DANIDA—TANWA groups. DANIDA is enthusiastic about formation of SHGs among the family members of Village Development Association formed for the smooth implementation of the watershed project so that there could be an integrated approach to the development of the area.

Sericulture SHGs

The department of sericulture on a pilot basis intends to form Quality Clubs called Seri 2000 in Coimbatore and Dharmapuri district. There will be 6-8 sericulturist members in each club and a group leader to co-ordinate the activity. The members will be taught the latest technique in drip irrigation, shoot harvesting and integrated pest and disease management in order to increase the production of mulberry leaves and boost output of silk worm cocoons which in turn will provide sustainable income of the silk worm breeders. The focus will be on voluntary participation and formation of SHGs while personnel from the Sericulture Department will be the technical facilitators. In course of time, the sericulture department intends to increase the number of groups to cover all sericulture farmers throughout Tamil Nadu.

SUMMARY

Thus Government and Non-Governmental Agencies have made multifarious attempts to promote Self Help Groups. Serious and intensive efforts are being taken by NABARD in promoting capacity building of NGOs, encouraging and supporting innovations like SHG Federations, NGO Networking, replication of Bangladesh Grameen Bank Model, Community Development Societies approach, based on the experience in Kerala Credit Union, RRB as Self Help Promoting Institutions and other local initiatives based on sound principles of micro finance.

3

Review of Literature

INTRODUCTION

Providing women with financial credit and helping them to set up small enterprises thus enabling them to increase their earning is considered as a means of poverty reduction and economic empowerment. Many NGOs have initiated the empowerment process of poor women by organising them into groups and building their capacity to improve their lives through micro credit programme. Evaluation is undertaken to know how the programme is being implemented and what can be done to remove the constraints, if any. Evaluation is thus a kind of achievement audit and mostly takes place after the programme has run for some specific period.

It is desirable to review the relevant literature while handling a research problem. A review of literature places a research study in its proper perspective by showing the amount of work already carried out in the related areas of the study.

REVIEW OF PREVIOUS STUDIES

The following are the studies which enabled the researcher to undertake this study.

Puhazhendi (1995) studied 19 SHGs and five bank branches in Karnataka and Tamil Nadu and concluded that the intermediation of SHGs reduced the time spent by bank personnel in identification of borrowers, documentation, follow up and recoveries effecting 40 per cent reduction in the transaction cost of bank, as compared to direct lending to individual borrowers. Transaction cost of borrowers was reduced by 85 per cent.[1]

Indian Bank (1995) had conducted a similar study in Tamil Nadu, covering 45 branches of their bank and 101 SHGs. The study examined only the transaction costs of the branches under different models for credit delivered for medium team loans upto Rs. 25,000. It concluded that lending to SHGs, which on-lend to borrowers with NGO acting as non-financial intermediary, resulted in saving of transaction costs to the extent of 45 per cent as compared to lending under government sponsored programmes and other direct lending projects.[2]

The Bank Performance improvement study under the Maharashtra Rural Credit Project (MRCP) concluded that with SHG intermediation, the transaction and risk costs of the advances of the rural branches could be brought down that could help turn around many loss making rural branches (BIRD, 1996).[3]

Hemalatha Prasad (1997) of the National Institute of Rural Development, Hyderabad carried out two case studies, one in Salem district of Tamil Nadu and another in Tribal Development Project areas of Andhra Pradesh to understand the process of economic empowerment of women. In Salem district 11 blocks were covered under (IFAD) International Fund for Agricultural Development Programme. This project broadly envisaged empowering rural women by expanding their resources, improving access to credit, rising the level of awareness, better access to health and establishment of a viable model for women's development.

The findings of the study revealed that the intermediate objective of social enhancement through group dynamics and the bringing of rural women into the mainstream of credit delivery seems to have been achieved with reasonable success. In Andhra Pradesh a case study on "Thrift Society and Grain Bank for Economic Empowerment Tribal Women" was conducted at Vampaliguda village, Srikakulam district. The main objective of this study was to improve the household food security and to promote sustainable self reliance amongst the participant groups. The study observed that the making of women's societies responsible for construction of school buildings, check dams and satellite nurseries resulted in the capacity build up of the women concern. The long term objective of inculcating saving habit and building up food security have, however not been achieved.[4]

Girija and Satish (1999) in their study on impact of SHG lending on the profitability of branches studied eight branches where the SHG lending constituted more than five per cent of the loan port folio. They concluded that lending to SHGs and NGOs carried the least cost when compared with other models of lending. Lending through SHGs reduced the costs by 85 per cent and through a federation, reduced the costs by 95 per cent as compared to direct lending. The default risk was negligible in the case of lending to SHG and NGO/federation.[5]

The National Bank for Agriculture and Rural Development (NABARD, 2000) conducted a study on the impact of Micro Finance (MF) on the living standards of SHGs members. The study aimed to find out how far the SHG bank linkage programme had lightened the burden of life for the average member of a SHG and to analysis the betterment of household by gaining access to micro finance. The study covered 560 SHG member households from 223 SHGs spread over 11 states. It showed positive results. There were perceptible and wholesome changes in the living standards of the SHG members, in terms of ownership of assets, increase in savings and borrowing capacity, income generating activities and income levels. The study revealed that almost all the members developed saving habits in the post-SHG situation as against 23 per cent of households who had this habit earlier and the average borrowings per year household increased from Rs. 4,282 to Rs. 8,341. The study concluded that the involvement in the group significantly contributed in improving the self-confidence of the members. The feelings of self-worth and communication with others improved after association with the SHGs and the members were relatively more assertive in confronting social evils and problem situation. As a result, there was a fall in the incidence of family violence.[6]

Mahab Sen (2000) has attempted a study to find out the development of SHGs promoted by Sreemamahiala Samity and its impact on women members. It was a study of 10 SHGs selected in Nadia district on a random sampling technique in July, 1999. The study included focus group discussion with the members of the SHGs in separate sessions followed by interview of 100 members through structured schedule. The findings of the study revealed that the individual loans were mostly used for productive purposes, the rate of recovery was very high compared to the rate of recovery of the formal institutional system and group dynamics was an instrument for change in the quality of life of the poor people. The study also revealed that other than economic activities, the groups worked towards primary education, basic health care of family, safe drinking water and environment protection. The study concluded that group cohesion, group action, need-based credit timely repayment are essential elements for sustainability of the groups.[7]

The study under review was a case study on "Environment of women through NGOs—The SEWA Bank experience". This study was done by Suman Jain (2000). The study observed that the bank (SEWA) (Self Employed Women's Association) had been providing banking services to the poor, illiterate, self-employed women and had become a viable financial venture. The case study revealed that there were 67113 women depositors with a working capital of Rs. 1916.72 lakhs in 1966. If further observed that the banks helped the women to acquire skills to make new products and identify work opportunities. It is also found that the repayment rate had been excellent, which was between 93 and 96 per cent due to close monitoring by the bank, the link between the group leaders and borrowers and constant communication between the bank and village group. The conclusion was that from the women's point, their involvement in and ownership of a successful institution enhanced their collective strength and empowerment that came with organisation. From a wider perspective, member-owned or controlled micro-credit institution could help to strengthen the country's democratic system.[8]

Kallur, M.S. and Biradar, A.A. (2000) in their micro level study aimed to examine the role of non-governmental voluntary organisations in promoting the micro-credit institutions and to comment on their sustainability in the years to come. The study was based on secondary data. The study has thrown light on the origin and the nature of micro-credit organisation and its superiority over macro ones in catering to the need of farmers. It also revealed that as a result of continuous efforts of NABARD, 255 groups linked together as on 31st March 1998 and had increased to 14,317 covering 30 commercial banks, 101 RRBs (Regional Rural Banks), 17 co-operative banks, 260 NGOs in 19 states and two union territories involving bank a loan of Rs. 23.62 crore and NABARD refinance of Rs. 21.38 crore. The study also discussed the role of micro-credit organisations with particular reference to the Indo-Swiss project and their sustainability and concluded that the NGOs have succeeded in promoting SHGs.[9]

Manimekalai, N. (2000) in her study on "NGOs" intervention through Micro Credit for Self Help Women Groups in Rural Tamil Nadu" had attempted to analyse the working of the SEVAI (Society of Education Village Action and Improvement) in empowering women and the rural poor through micro credit. The objectives of the study were to find out the characteristics and working of the micro-credit institution namely, Villuthukal. This was a bank established for the benefit of SHGs to assist them by extending micro credit and to highlight the strategies adopted to mobilise the women to form Self Help Groups. The study was based on primary and secondary data. The secondary data were collected from the records of SEVAI and the primary data were collected from 70 women who were the members and who had availed credit from the bank. The analysis of the study revealed that the women in rural areas were really longing for supplementary income and the intervention through micro credit, by both government, non-government organisations, would be a boon to them. The study also proved that, after the micro credit and intervention of SEVAI, the education of the children had been better cared for and the women-beneficiary households were able to manage the budget without deficit. The study concluded with the suggestion that micro credit strategies could be followed by other institutions working for the upliftment of women and prove that micro credit would be instrumental in realising the proposed objective.[10]

Choudhury, R.C. and his team (2001) conducted a study to document the experience of SHGs in promoting micro enterprises through micro-credit interventions and the efficacy of Self Help Promoting Institution (SHPI). The study analysed the core issue of poverty reduction and efficacy of SHG route for micro enterprise promotion. The main objective of the study were to analyse the operating system in SHGs, to explore the effectiveness of SHGs in identifying the micro enterprises and to suggest appropriate policy intervention for effective performance of SHGs. The study was carried out in selected clusters spread over regions in the states of Tamil Nadu, Karnataka, Andhra Pradesh and Maharashtra. The study covered 76 SHGs, 450 members and 135 micro entrepreneurs from five regions. The case study-cum-survey method was followed. Secondary data were also collected from the records of SHGs. It was observed that group enterprise on a big scale would involve greater risks but would yield better returns to the entrepreneurs. The study brought to the fore the fact that, out of three SHPIs namely, NGOs banks and government, NGOs were better equipped for capacity building of SHGs and promotion of micro-enterprises. The study also showed that SHG were still in a state of flux and their sustainable development depended on a number of factors which were internal and external to the organisation.[11]

Namboodiri, N.V. and R.L. Shiyani (2001) conducted a study to find out the basic features and financial operations of SHGs promoted by both SHPI and NGOs served by the Panchmahals Vadodara Grameen Bank (PVGB). A sample of five branches of PVGB were selected, out of which three are located in Dahod district and two in Panchmahals district, of Gujarat state. The main findings that emerged from this study were that, while the percentage of women groups promoted by the SHPI was 52 per cent, it was as high as 84 per cent for those promoted by the NGOs. The percentage of SHGs linked by the SHPI was 65 per cent and that of NGO was 42 per cent. The average amount advanced to SHGs varied from Rs. 7,000 to Rs. 30,000 for those promoted by the NGOs. The SHG that were promoted by the NGOs had a better saving performance compared to that of SHPI, in terms of amount saved per SHGs as well as in terms of credit saving ratio. The repayment performance of the SHGs promoted by the SHPI was superior to that of NGOs.[12]

Dadhich, C.L. (2001) conducted a case study of Oriental Bank Grameen Project at Dehradun district in Uttar Pradesh, for assessing the benefit of the project and economic viability. Out of a total 450 SHGs covered by the project, 447 were women groups and only 3 were men SHGs. The main findings of the study revealed that a large number of women had taken up subsidiary occupation and consequently their family incomes had substantially increased. An analysis of figures relating to income and expenditure of a specialised micro credit branch revealed that the branch had become a profit-centre right in the second year of its operation. The recovery of the loans was more than 100 per cent of the demand. The study also revealed that the borrowers under Oriental Bank Grameen Project had both the advantages of fine rate of interest, as well as hassle-free credit, whereas their counterparts elsewhere were paying exorbitant rates of interest.[13]

The objective of the Madheswaran, S. and Dharmadhikary Amita's (2001) study on "Empowering Rural Women Through SHGs" was to examine the SHG mechanism of the micro-credit scheme as an effective and financially viable tool in channelising credit to the rural poor. In this study an attempt had been made to analyse the impact of SHGs in providing credit to rural women, to help them to uplift their economic status. The analysis was based on a survey of three villages of Pune district, conducted during 1999, where the Maharashtra Rural Credit Programme was being implemented. The study revealed that the Maharashtra Rural Credit Programme was successful to some extent in its objective due to a combination of factors such as: (i) SHG-Bank linkage; (ii) Credit being made available for consumption purposes; (iii) easy and periodic availability of credit due to rotation of savings; (iv) active participation of the NGOs. The study further revealed that peer monitoring could be used as a channel to provide credit at a low transaction cost and frequently to reduce rural poverty. The study concluded that micro credit should be used to meet the current demands of the rural women and this should lead to gradual improvement in the quality of their life and would enable them to identify activities for economic betterment.[14]

Satis, P. (2001) in his study made an attempt to answer the following questions (i) Are there a large number of pre existing groups in the rural areas and if so can they evolve into suitable SHGs? (ii) Are the really poor accepted as members of SHGs? (iii) What are the processes in SHG formation? (iv) Do the SHGs face resistance at the time of their formation, if so how is the resistance being overcome? This study covered groups formed by the NGOs and banks. The number of groups formed by the NGOs and banks were five and four respectively in Karnataka, four and nil in Maharashtra and seven and two in Uttar Pradesh. These groups were selected for the study. The secondary data and material were collected over the period 1997 to 2000 at the Bankers Institute of Rural Development (BIRD, Lucknow).

The study revealed that several SHGs included very poor members and the process of SHG formation had to be systematic whether it was formed by a bank or an NGO. It also observed that most of the SHGs had faced initial resistance in their efforts. The study concluded that the NGOs were more suited for forming and nurturing the SHGs.[15]

The National Institute of Bank Management (NIBM, 2001) has studied SHG in four district of Maharashtra promoted under Maharashtra Rural Credit Project (MRCP). The study observed that 69 per cent of the groups were of the size 11-20, 50 per cent of the members were illiterate. The study further observed that 55 per cent of the office bearers had at least a secondary level of education. The study revealed that the average savings of the SHGs in MRCP was Rs. 24 per month per member. This rate was more for new groups than for the old groups. The study also found that the average amount of savings mobilised amounted to Rs. 10,658 per group and that the SHGs and MRCP had started lending their own thrift capital from the eighth month of the formation.[16]

Lalitha, N. and B. S. Nagarjan (2002) conducted a critical study on the functioning of the self help groups (SHGs) in selected districts of Tamil Nadu. The study was undertaken to document the efforts of NGOs in promoting SHGs. The objectives of the study were to trace the structure and modalities of Self Help Groups, study the functioning of the SHGs, examine the role of SHG in promoting empowerment of women, investigate the group dynamics of SHGs, identify the factors which contributed to the success/failure of the groups and study the income generating programmes promoted by SHGs. The study was based on multistage sampling technique. It had been carried out in three districts. NGOs who had organised SHGs for more than four years were identified. Out of the 14 institutions, nine NGOs were selected and two SHGs from each NGO were selected on the basis of non-proportionate random sampling method. The study was based on survey method and had covered both secondary and primary data. The study highlighted the facts that SHGs were people's institutions and with their support, the women could march towards empowerment and that the groups could promote individual and groups ventures of income generating activities under the effective guidance of NGOs. The study also revealed that effective leadership, group cohesiveness, savings, regular meetings, peer-group pressure, linkage with other institutions and effective supervision by the NGOs were the factors which contributed to the success of the groups.[17]

Sudha Rani, K., D. Umadevi and G. Surendra (2002) had undertaken a study to evaluate the social status of women in house management, leadership qualities, health and sanitation and economic status after participation in the Self Help Groups. Out of 600 Self Help Groups established by Padmavathi Mahila Mandal, Tirupati, Andhra Pradesh, 50 Self Help Groups were randomly selected for the study. From each group selected two women members were selected randomly. The study was based on primary data and a specially designed rating scale was administered to the sample to collect the information. The findings of the study revealed that, in all the four aspects there was positive correlation between the women's educational status and empowerment. The study observed that the participation in SHGs enhanced the empowerment of women in these four aspects. Self-confidence among the women increased. Their decision-making power also increased during the period of participation.

SUMMARY

In the light of the studies reviewed above, the importance and need for in-depth and comprehensive action research on SHGs and Micro Credit becomes highly significant and socially and economically beneficial.

REFERENCES

1. Puhazhendhi, V., (1995), "Transaction Costs of Lending to the Rural Poor—NGOs and SHGs of the Poor as Intermediaries for Banks in India", *The Foundation for Development Corporation*, Australia: Brisbane.

2. Indian Bank (1995), "Performance of Indian Bank Branches in SHG Lending", *Rural Banker*, Issue No. 21, p. 2.

3. Bankers Institute for Rural Development, (1996), "Bank Performance Improvement under Maharashtra Rural Credit Project", *Rural Banker*, Issue No. 21, p. 22.

4. Prasad Hemalatha, (1998), "IFAD's (International Fund for Agricultural Development) Women's Development Programme for Economic Empowerment" in Sushama Sahay (eds.) (1998), *Women and Empowerment—Approaches and Strategies*, New Delhi: Discovery Publishing House, pp. 170-172.

5. Srinivasan, Girija and Satish (1999), "Impact of SHG Lending on the Profitability of Branches", *Rural Banker*, Issue No. 21, p. 22.

6. National Bank for Agriculture for Rural Development (NABARD), (2000), *Report on Impact of Micro Finance on the Living Standards of SHG Members*, 1999-2000, Mumbai.

7. Sen, Manab (2000), "Self Help Groups and Micro Finance: An Alternative Socio Economic Option for the Poor", in Kamta Prasad (eds.) (2000), *NGO's and Socio Economic Development Opportunities*, New Delhi: Deep and Deep Publication Pvt. Ltd., pp. 77-89.

8. Jain, Suman (2000), "Empowerment of Women through NGOs—The SEWA Bank Experience", in Kamta Prasad (eds.) (2000), *NGO's and Socio Economic Development Opportunities*, New Delhi: Deep and Deep Publication Pvt. Ltd., pp. 112-119.

9. Kallur, M.S. and A.A. Biradar, (2000), "The New Paradigm of Micro Finance and the Role of Non-governmental Voluntary Agencies in its Promotion: A Few Reflections" in Kamta Prasad (eds.) (2000), *NGO's and Socio Economic Development Opportunities*, New Delhi: Deep and Deep Publication Pvt. Ltd., pp. 67-75.

10. Manimekalai, N. (2000), "NGO's Intervention through Micro Credit for Self Help Women Groups in Rural Tamil Nadu", in Kamta Prasad (eds.) (2000), *NGO's and Socio Economic Development Opportunities*, New Delhi: Deep and Deep Publication Pvt. Ltd., pp. 96-110.

11. Choudhury, R.C. and N. Mohan, (2001), "Micro Enterprises Development and SHGs", *Micro Credit for Micro Enterprises*, Hyderabad: National Institute of Rural Development, pp. 89-143.

12. Namboodiri, N.V. and R.L. Shiyani, (2001), "Potential Role of SHGs in Rural Financial Deepening", *Indian Journal of Agriculture Economics*, Vol. 56, No. 3, July-Sep., pp. 401-405.

13. Dadhich, C.L. (2001), "Micro Finance—A Panacea for Poverty Alleviation: A Case Study of Oriental Grameen Project in India", *Indian Journal of Agriculture Economics*, Vol. 56, No. 3, July-Sep., pp. 419-420.

14. Madheswaran, S. and Amita Dharmadhikasy (2001), "Empowering Rural Women through SHGs: Lessons from Maharashtra Rural Credit Project", *Indian Journal of Agriculture Economics*, Vol. 56, No. 3, July-Sep., pp. 398-400.

15. Satish, P. (2001), "Some Issues in the Formation of Self Help Groups", Working Paper Published in *Indian Journal of Agriculture Economics*, Vol. 56, No. 3, July-Sep., pp. 410-416.

16. National Institute of Bank Management (NIBM) (2001), "Maharashtra Rural Credit Project (MRCP)", *Indian Journal of Agriculture Economics*, Vol. 56, No. 3, July-Sep., pp. 400-402.

17. Lalitha, N. and B.S. Nagarajan (2002), "Functioning of the SHGs in Selected District of Tamil Nadu", (eds.), *Self Help Groups in Rural Development*, New Delhi: Dominant Publishers and Distributors.

18. Sudha Rani, K. and D. Umadevi, (2002), "SHGs Micro Credit and Empowerment", *Social Welfare*, February, pp. 20-22.

4

Methodology

The methodology of this study was designed in tune with the objectives set, as a detailed hereunder:

— Organising women at grassroots into Self Help Groups (SHGs);

— Motivating the SHGs to undertake income generation activities, availing the micro-credit facilities in experience; and

— Evaluating the impact of micro-credit utilisation by the SHGs.

ORGANISING WOMEN AT GRASSROOTS INTO SELF HELP GROUPS

This process was carried out under the following headings:

(i) Selecting the locale

(ii) Motivating women to organise SHGs

(iii) Encouraging women to mobilise thrift and credit activities.

(i) Selecting the Locale

The Department of Women and Child Development, Ministry of Human Resource Development, Government of India, entrusted the responsibility of organising and implementing the New Indira Mahila Yojana (IMY) in Coimbatore district to the Avinashilingam Education Trust Institution (with the NGO status), which had established its credibility in working with women for over three decades. The researcher was put in charge of co-ordinating this project by the trust. Six slums from Coimbatore corporation and five villages from Karamadai Block of Coimbatore district, where Avinashilingam Trust Institutions had formed Indira Mahila Kendras (IMK) were selected for initiating the SHGs.

(ii) Motivating Women to Organise SHGs

The leaders of the slums in the urban areas and of the villages were met regularly to explain the concept of SHGs and their advantages. A discussion meeting was arranged with the manager of the Lead Bank, Canara Bank, Coimbatore, who also enlightened the leaders of the conditions laid down by the NABARD that women have to organise themselves into SHGs to become eligible for credit support from banks. The leaders were oriented on the modalities of formation of SHGs and initiating thrift and credit activities. A booklet was prepared in local languages to offer guidelines to the members.

The procedure for on-lending in terms of the number of members to be given the loan, rate of interest and repayment schedule was left to the discretion of the groups concerned. Pass books were printed and distributed to the members of the SHGs. The bank managers of the respective areas were approached for opening accounts in the name of the SHGs.

The women were trained to conduct group meetings, keep accounts calculate interest and work out the repayment schedule.

In accordance with the mandate of the project, 20 SHGs each in the Coimbatore Corporation Slums (urban) and Karamadai Panchayat Union (Rural) were formed by the researcher after establishing rapport with the community and motivating the leaders. The urban SHGs (six slums) recruited 358 members, while 357 women became members of SHGs in the rural areas (five villages) (Table—4.1).

Table—4.1 Village-wise distribution of the SHGs and the members

S. No.	Areas/Villages	Number of SHGs	Number of Members
A.	**Urban—Coimbatore Corporation Slums**		
1.	Avarampalayam	5	90
2.	Karuppuswamy Nagar	3	55
3.	Periyar Nagar	4	80
4.	Seeranaicken Palayam	2	31
5.	Selvapuram	4	67
6.	Shanmuga Nagar	2	35
	Total	**20**	**358**
B.	**Rural—Karamadai Panchayat Union**		
1.	Chellapanur	3	60
2.	Karamadai	8	137
3.	Sastri Nagar	4	70
4.	Tholampalayam	2	35
5.	Vellingadu	3	55
	Total	**20**	**357**

(iii) Encouraging the Group to Mobilise Thrift and Credit Activities

Every group (SHG) has selected its own leader. The amount to be saved was decided upon by the group, which ranged from Rs. 30 to Rs. 50 per head per month.

MOTIVATING THE SHGs TO UNDERTAKE INCOME GENERATING ACTIVITIES AVAILING THE MICRO CREDIT FACILITIES

This aspect of the study is dealt with under the following headings:

(i) Interaction with the SHGs;

(ii) Selection of micro enterprises;

(iii) Training the micro entrepreneurs in vocational skills and credit management;

(iv) Availing the micro credit facilities; and

(v) Undertaking income generating activities.

(i) Interaction with the SHGs

After forming the SHGs, several focus group meetings were conducted to elicit the needs and interests of the group members with regard to income generating activities. The socio-economic background of the women was also studied. Such interactions revealed that 121 urban and 133 rural SHG members were ready to undertake micro enterprises.

(ii) Selection of Micro Enterprises

In accordance with the background of the SHGs members and keeping in view the financial implications and marketability of the products, income generating activities were selected. The income generating activities pertained to four sectors namely, agriculture/ allied, manufacturing, trading and servicing.

(iii) Training the Micro Entrepreneurs in Vocational Skills and Credit Management

The following training programmes were arranged for the prospective micro entrepreneurs:

(a) Vocational skill training;

(b) Preparation of simple business plans; and

(c) Credit management.

(a) Vocational Skill Training

Utilising the infrastructure of the Trust namely, Avinashilingam Jan Shikshan Sansthan, Avinashilingam Trainer's Training Centre and Avinashilingam Krishi Vigyana Kendra, 37 women from urban and 51 women from rural areas, who opted for production-type of enterprises, were given vocational skill training namely, in detergent making, catering, cottage industries and tailoring.

(b) Preparation of Simple Business Plans

The prospective micro entrepreneurs were oriented by the researcher on how to prepare simple and viable business plans keeping in view the raw materials and infrastructure available, finance required, marketing facilities and other details.

(c) Credit Management

The micro entrepreneurs were trained in credit management in terms of costing, account keeping, profit calculation, etc. Thrust was given to developing desirable repayment behaviour right from the inception.

(iv) Availing the Micro Credit Facilities

To begin with, the SHG members were motivated to carry out internal lending (i.e. among the group members) out of the savings mobilised by the groups. The terms and conditions for such internal lending were decided in the group meetings under the direction of the researcher.

In the meantime, the bankers were oriented by the researcher on the modalities of operation of SHGs and the need for micro credit. The SHG members were also encouraged to approach the banks with viable business plans for availing micro credit. As a result five nationalised banks agreed to offer micro facilities to the SHGs. In addition, loans were also given from the revolving loan fund scheme of the Avinashilingam Education Trust—a corpus fund created to help women in need.

(v) Undertaking the Income Generation Activities

Table—4.2 gives the details of income generation activities undertaken by the SHG members:

There were 12 categories of micro enterprises spread under four sectors namely, agriculture/allied, manufacturing, trading and servicing.

It can be seen from Table—4.2 that the urban area entrepreneurs preferred enterprises such as poultry in the agricultural sector, detergent-making in the manufacturing sector, sale of cloth in the trading sector and grinding in the servicing sector. Whereas the rural entrepreneurs preferred mostly diary farming in agriculture sector, cottage industry in manufacturing sector, sale of food items/catering in trading sector and tailoring in servicing sector.

Table—4.2 Details of income generation activities undertaken by the SHG members

(No. of members)

S. No.	Area	No. of entrepreneurs	*Agricultural and allied sector*				*Manufacturing sector*				*Trading sector*				*Servicing sector*			
			Dairy farming	*Polutry*	*Sheep goat rearing*	*Sub total*	*Cottage industries*	*Detergent making*	*Food process/catering*	*Sub total*	*Petty shop*	*Sale of cloth*	*Sale of food items*	*Sub total*	*Tailoring*	*Grinding*	*Laundry*	*Sub total*
1.	Urban	121 (47.64)	3 (30.00)	7 (87.50)	2 (40.00)	12 (52.17)	9 (39.13)	16 (80.00)	10 (29.41)	35 (45.95)	20 (54.05)	28 (60.87)	15 (31.91)	63 (48.46)	2 (18.18)	5 (83.33)	4 (57.14)	11 (45.83)
2.	Rural	133 (52.36)	7 (70.00)	1 (12.50)	3 (60.00)	11 (47.83)	14 (20.00)	4 (70.59)	24 (54.55)	42 (45.95)	17 (45.95)	18 (39.13)	32 (68.09)	67 (51.54)	9 (81.82)	1 (16.67)	3 (42.86)	13 (54.17)
	Total	254 (100.00)	10 (100.00)	8 (100.00)	5 (100.00)	23 (100.00)	23 (100.00)	20 (100.00)	34 (100.00)	77 (100.00)	37 (100.00)	46 (100.00)	47 (100.00)	130 (100.00)	11 (100.00)	6 (100.00)	7 (100.00)	24 (100.00)

Note: Figures in bracket denote percentage to total.

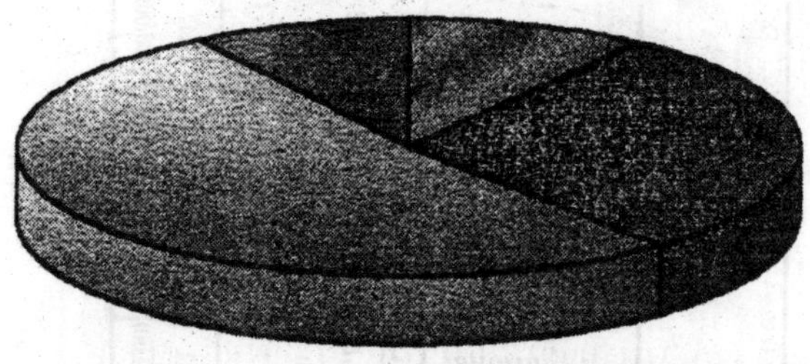

Fig. 4.1: Income Generation Activities both in the Urban and Rural Areas

Only 12 out of 121 members in urban areas and 11 out of 133 members in the rural opted for the agricultural sector. It was observed that out of 121 urban entrepreneurs, 63 of them preferred trading business and out of 133 rural entrepreneurs, 67 of them preferred trading business. Of the total of 254 members, 130 preferred the trading sector, 77 the manufacturing sector, 24 opted for the servicing sector and 23 preferred agricultural business. Trading business predominated the income generation activities both in the urban and rural settings (Figure 4.1).

EVALUATING THE IMPACT OF MICRO CREDIT UTILISATION BY THE SHG MEMBERS IN QUANTITATIVE AND QUALITATIVE DIMENSIONS

The impact of the micro credit utilisation by the SHGs was assessed on the following lines:

(i) Overall performance of the SHGs;

(ii) Economic returns from the micro enterprises undertaken;

(iii) Social benefits accrued to the members of the SHGs; and

(iv) Appraisal of the strengths and weaknesses of the SHGs in micro credit management.

(i) Overall Performance of the SHGs

This aspect of the evaluation was done to study the following:

- profile of the members of the SHGs;
- flow of savings mobilised by the SHGs; and
- lending operations carried out by the SHGs.

The data was collected from:

(a) *Primary Sources* namely, interview schedules administered to the members and leaders of the SHGs under study; and

(b) *Secondary Sources* namely, the records and monthly statements maintained by the groups, such as cash book, loan ledger, savings register, minutes book of the meetings conducted, members' attendance registers and bank pass book.

(ii) Economic Returns from the Micro Enterprises Undertaken

This part of the evaluation was done to elicit the details as given hereunder:

(a) Incremental income realised from the different micro enterprises

(b) Assets created

(c) Employment generated

(d) Relationship between investment in micro enterprises and incremental income, employment generated and assets created

(e) Repayment behaviour of the micro entrepreneurs.

The *incremental income* realised was assessed in terms of:

- Mean increase in household income for the micro entrepreneurs
- Income variation rate
- Shift of the households above poverty line
- Shift of the households to higher income groups
- Various sources of finance influencing the incremental income
- Investment income ratio

The *assets created* were estimated in terms of the machinery, tools and equipment, furniture, animals purchased, etc., by the micro entrepreneurs concerned. The *employment generated* was assessed based on the increase in man-days of work. The relationship between the investment incurred and the incremental income, assets created and employment generated was also examined using the data pertaining to all the above elicited through interview schedules administered to the micro-entrepreneurs at the pre-credit and post-credit periods, supplemented through discussions and observations for reliability and viability. The schedule was first prepared in English for the pilot study and in the light of pilot study, the schedule was revised. The interview schedule was, then translated into the local language for the convenience of the respondents.

(iii) Social Benefits Accrued to the Members of the SHGs

This part of the research included the following aspects:

(a) group dynamics of the SHGs; and

(b) degree of empowerment traits attained by the micro entrepreneurs.

The *group dynamics* of SHGs was assessed in terms of participation of members and collective action and articulation through a score card specially developed for the purpose.

The *empowerment* traits attained by the micro-entrepreneurs was estimated again through a score card administered to the women at the pre- and post-credit periods.

(iv) Appraisal of the Strengths and Weaknesses of the SHGs in Micro Credit Management

SWOT analysis was done to assess the strong as well as the weak points of the SHGs in micro credit management and the opportunities and threats.

S	W
O	T

This SWOT analysis was carried out on eighty women representing all categories of the micro enterprises initiated.

REFERENCE PERIOD

As the study aims at analysing the performance of micro-credit programme in the pre- and post-framework; it was felt that the reference period selected should be such that it would allow sufficient time for the programme to have its full impact on the economic conditions of the beneficiaries. Considering this, the reference period had been fixed as 1999-2000. Thus, those respondents who obtained the assistance either at the end of 1996-97 or at the beginning of 1997-98, had been selected and subsequently, a pilot visit to the areas revealed that the women started gaining income only during the year 1997-98. Therefore, the year 1996-97 had been considered as the base year to assess the pre micro credit income and the year 1999-2000 as the reference period.

To understand the various aspects of implementation of the programme, the investigator underwent a special training programme on "Credit and Micro Enterprises" (CRÈME) for the implementation of Indira Mahila Yojana" at Durham Business School, Durham University, United Kingdom, from April 7, 1997 to June 10, 1997, sponsored by the British Council and Department of Women and Child Development, Government of India. The researcher also attended a training on the same at Bankers Institute for Rural Development, Lucknow, from 15th to 28th February 1997. The investigator also participated in the Asian Pacific Micro Credit Summit held at New Delhi from 1st to 5th February 2001, organised by All India Women's Conference, New Delhi, Asian Development Bank, Manila and Micro Credit Summit, Washington DC.

TOOLS FOR ANALYSIS

The following tools were used for analysis of the data collected:

(i) Paired 't' test;

(ii) Correlation analysis;

(iii) Regression analysis;

(iv) Multiple regression analysis; and

(v) Ration analysis.

(i) Paired 't' Test

Paired 't' test was employed to compare the variation in generation of income, asset position and employment generation of the members for the various micro enterprises of four sectors namely, agriculture and allied manufacturing, training and servicing, financed by different sources between the base year and post credit year.

(ii) Correlation Analysis

Correlation analysis technique was used to analyse the relationship between the variables such as investment and income, investment and asset position, investment and employment generation, age of SHG and the average saving per member, age of the group and the average loan per member.

(iii) Regression Analysis

Regression analysis model was used to study the impact of investment on asset position of the micro entrepreneurs.

(iv) Multiple Regression Analysis

Multiple regression analysis was used to study the various sources of credit and the other determinants influencing the incremental income of the SHG members and also to study the impact of SHGs on the SHG net income per member.

- To study the sources of credit on the average household income of the members, the average household income of the members was taken as an dependent variable and the explanatory variables were SHGs, scheduled banks, corpus fund, friends and relatives and moneylenders of Avinashilingam Education Trust Institution.
- To find out the major determinants influencing the incremental income of the members, average, incremental income of the member was considered as a dependent variable. The explanatory variables were average loan, average own funds, average incremental assets, average incremental mandays, average interest paid, average incremental household expenses, average educational level of entrepreneurs.
- To study the impact of SHGs on the SHG net income per member, dependent variable was SHG net income per member and the explanatory variables were average distance between members in SHGs, average educational level of members in the SHGs, average loan provided, age of SHGs, and the percentage share of SHGs expenditure in the total income of SHGs.

(v) Ratio Analysis

The following ratios were used for assessing the performance of the SHGs and incremental income realised by the micro enterprises:

(i) Recovery Index

(ii) Thrift Credit Ratio/Velocity of Internal Lending

(iii) Rate of Outstanding on Total Loans

(iv) Investment Income Ratio

(v) Portfolio in arrears ratio

(i) Recovery Index

The recovery index arrived at is as follows:

$$\frac{\text{Amount recovered}}{\text{Demand for recovery}} \times 100$$

(ii) Velocity of Internal Lending

This ratio is calculated as follows:

$$\frac{\text{Total loans disbursed}}{\text{Total savings mobilised}}$$

(iii) Outstanding Loans in Percentage

Outstanding loans in percentage was arrived at is as follows:

$$\frac{\text{Total lending-Demand for recovery}}{\text{Total lending}} \times 100$$

(iv) Investment Income Ratio

Investment income ratio is calculated as follows:

$$\frac{\text{Mean income}}{\text{Mean investment}} \times 100$$

Investment includes (loans and own funds)

(v) Port-folio in Arrears Ratio

This is calculated by using the formula:

$$\frac{\text{Payment over due}}{\text{Payments outstanding}} \times 100$$

Besides the above mentioned tools of analysis, percentage, means standard deviation, co-efficient of variation, chi-square test, graphs and diagrams were used wherever necessary. In-depth, analysis was done to compare the findings in the urban and rural areas and also the categories of micro enterprises in different sectors.

5

Performance of the Self Help Groups

INTRODUCTION

Self Help Groups have been formed in the urban slums and villages of rural areas with the assumption that, whenever a homogeneous group of poor people shares an environment and common needs, they are bound to take up activities jointly, which are meant for the welfare of the whole group. This chapter deals with the performance of the SHGs formed by the researcher under Indira Mahila Yojana in Coimbatore district. Performance details were done with the help of the books and registers maintained by the groups and the information given by the group leaders and the members. This chapter is discussed under the following headings.

- Profile of SHG members
- Thrift and credit activities of the SHGs
- Credit flow realised
- Regression analysis of SHGs

PROFILE OF SHG MEMBERS

The profile of the members of the SHGs in the urban and rural areas is furnished in Table—5.1.

A large majority of 90.5 per cent from the urban slums and 83.29 per cent from the rural areas belonged to the Hindu religion. While the backward castes were more prevalent inthe rural areas (53.78 per cent), the scheduled caste (65.65 per cent) predominated in the urban areas.

Table—5.1 Profile of SHG members

Details	Percentage	
	Urban (N : 358)	Rural (N : 357)
1. Religion		
Hindu	90.50	83.29
Muslim	6.98	10.07
Christian	2.52	6.64
2. Caste		
Backward	7.82	53.78
Most backward	26.53	26.62
Scheduled caste	65.65	19.60
3. Type of family		
Nuclear	72.90	85.72
Joint	27.10	14.28
4. Size of the family		
1–4	67.04	85.15
5 and above	32.96	14.85
5. Age of the members in years		
Below 30	14.25	15.40
31–40	52.79	58.82
41 and above	32.96	25.78
6. Educational status of the members		
Illiterate	30.17	40.62
Primary	25.69	24.08
Middle	22.35	17.92
Secondary	15.37	12.33
Higher secondary	4.18	3.93
Graduate	2.24	1.12
7. Annual income of the family (Rs.)		
Below 5,000	33.52	36.14
5,000–10,000	53.64	51.26
10,001–11,500	1.12	4.48
11,501–13,600	4.18	5.88
13,601 and above	7.54	2.24

About 72.9 per cent members from the urban areas and 85.72 per cent from the rural streams hailed from nuclear types of families, reflecting the national trend. The size of the families was small, i.e. 1-4 for 67.04 per cent in the urban and 85.15 per cent in the rural areas.

As for as literacy status, the rural areas appeared to be worse with 40.62 per cent illiterate women against 30.17 per cent in the urban areas. Among the literates, the maximum number of women had studied upto the secondary level in both the areas. A large majority of 52.79 per cent in the urban and 58.82 per cent in the rural areas were in the age group of 31-40 years and were settled in life. With regard to the annual income of the families, 92.46 per cent from the urban slum and 97.76 per cent from the rural areas were below the poverty line. As per the 9th plan, a person is said to be below the poverty line when his annual income is less than Rs. 13,680 for rural areas and Rs. 15,840 for urban areas (Narshian and Reddy, 1999).

THRIFT AND CREDIT ACTIVITIES OF THE SHGs

The activities of the selected self-help credit management groups were basically related to the promotion of thrift among the members with income generation and asset creation efforts. The saving and lending procedures adopted by groups were very simple and were based on mutual trust and confidence of the members. As a democratic body, all the members had equal opportunity to express their opinions. Decisions were to be made unanimously after thorough discussion among themselves. The purpose of loans provided was need-based and prioritisation among different purposes and members was collectively decided. The details of thrift and credit activities of the SHGs is dealt with under the following sub-headings:

1. Reasons for forming SHGs
2. Motives in joining the SHGs
3. Quantum and level of savings
4. Sources of income for thrift
5. Details of internal lending

(i) Reasons for forming SHGs

Table—5.2 gives the reasons mentioned by the members for forming the Self-Help Groups.

Table—5.2 Reasons for forming SHGs

S. No.	Reasons	Urban Area		Rural Area		Total	
		No. of groups (N: 20)	% to total	No. of groups (N: 20)	% to total	No. of groups (N: 40)	% to total
1.	To improve the economic and social status of the members	16	80	15	75	31	77.50
2.	To promote thrift and lending among the members	7	35	14	70	21	52.50
3.	To finance support from NGOs and the financial institutions	12	60	18	90	30	75.00
4.	To initiate income generation and asset creation efforts	20	100	20	100	40	100.00
5.	To take up community development activities	12	60	5	25	17	42.50

(Figures given in the column relate to multiple responses evinced by the groups).

It has been noted that 80 per cent of the groups in the urban areas reported that they initiated the groups in order to improve the economic and social conditions of their members, 35 per cent of the groups stated that they joined the groups solely to promote and develop thrift and lending among the members. Sixty per cent of the groups were started only to avail loans from other financial institutions, 100 per cent to start income generation activities and 60 per cent to take up community development programme.

In the case of rural areas, 75 per cent of the groups had started just to improve the economic status of the members. Seventy per cent reported that they were commenced to promote thrift among the members. A majority of the groups had been started to avail loans from other financial institutions such as, banks, Rashtriya Mahila Kosh and under Government schemes, including IRDP and DWCRA. However, the common objectives of starting the groups were stated by all of them as income generation and creation of assets. Only 25 per cent of the groups had been initiated to take up community development programmes.

(ii) Motives in Joining the SHGs

Prime motives for joining SHGs as stated by its members is presented in Table—5.3.

Table—5.3 Prime motives stated by members for joining the SHGs

S. No.	*Reasons*	*Urban (N : 358)*		*Rural (N : 357)*		*Total (N : 715)*	
		No. of members	*Percentage to total*	*No. of members*	*Percentage to total*	*No. of members*	*Percentage to total*
1.	To obtain credit	337	94.13	342	95.80	679	94.97
2.	From savings habit	302	84.36	328	91.88	630	88.11
3.	To meet unexpected expenditure	156	43.58	125	35.01	281	39.30
4.	Domestic demand	295	82.40	340	95.24	635	88.81
5.	Persuaded by others	308	86.03	327	91.60	635	88.81
6.	Access to bank credit	292	81.56	335	93.84	627	87.69
7.	Socio-economic empowerment	302	84.36	315	88.24	617	86.29

(Figures given in the column relate to multiple responses given by the members).

It is observed that a majority of the members (94.97 per cent) conceded that obtaining credit has been one of the prime motives for joining SHGs. This is followed by other reasons like fostering the savings habit (88.11 per cent), domestic demand (88.81 per cent), persuasion by others (88.81 per cent), access to bank credit (87.69 per cent), socio-economic empowerment (86.29 per cent) and meeting unexpected expenditure (39.30 per cent).

(iii) Quantum and Level of Savings

The amount saved every month is detailed in Table—5.4.

Table—5.4 Amount of savings

S. No.	Thrift collected per head per month	Urban Area		Rural Area		Total	
		No. of groups (N : 20)	% to total	No. of groups (N : 20)	% to total	No. of groups (N : 20)	% to total
1.	Rs. 30	–	–	16	80	16	40
2.	Rs. 50	20	100	4	20	24	60
	Total	**20**	**100**	**20**	**100**	**40**	**100**

The quantum of money saved by the members ranged from Rs. 30 to Rs. 50 per head per month. In the rural areas a large majority of 80 per cent of the groups saved Rs. 30 per head per month and the remaining 15 per cent of the groups saved Rs. 50 per head per month. All the members in the urban groups saved Rs. 50 per head per month.

Table—5.5 given the level of savings reached by the groups. The level of savings is calculated as follows:

$$\frac{\text{Actual savings mobilised}}{\text{Common savings rate x number of members x age of the group}} \text{ x } 100$$

Table—5.5 Level of savings

S No.	Level in percentage	Urban Area		Rural Area		Total	
		No. of groups (N : 20)	% to total	No. of groups (N : 20)	% to total	No. of groups (N : 40)	% to total
1.	Less than 90	–	–	–	–	–	–
2.	90-99	1	5	1	5	2	5
3.	100	19	95	19	95	38	95
	Total	**20**	**100**	**20**	**100**	**40**	**100**

It has been noted that 95 per cent of the groups, both in urban and rural areas, reached 100 per cent level of savings, which is highly remarkable, this shows that the members in these groups were regular and prompt in contributing their savings. Only five per cent of the groups, that is, only one group each from the urban area and the rural sector, reached the level of 90-99 per cent savings.

(iv) Sources of Income for Thrift

Thrift is one of the foundations of SHG edifices. Sources of income of thrift contributions made by SHG members are reported in Table—5.6.

Table—5.6 Sources of income of thrift contribution made by SHGs members in the study area

S. No.	Item	Urban Area (N : 358)		Rural Area (N : 357)		Total (N : 715)	
		Number	% to total	Number	% to total	Number	% to total
1.	Own labour	265	74.02	298	83.47	563	78.14
2.	Husband wage	78	21.79	45	12.61	123	17.20
3.	Livestock	13	3.63	10	2.80	23	3.22
4.	Others	2	0.56	4	1.12	6	0.84
	Total	358	100.00	357	100.00	715	100.00

It is seen that income from own labour was the major source (78.74 per cent) towards thrift contribution; followed by husband's wage (17 per cent), livestock (3.22 per cent) and others (0.84 per cent).

(v) Details of Internal Lending

(a) *Lending Norms*

It was learnt from the members of SHGs that some members borrowed a huge amount of money from SHGs for various domestic purposes, such as water and sewage connection, repairing of house and house construction. A large number of borrowers utilised the loan for business purposes, such as, setting up petty shop, fruit stalls, dairy farming, sheep rearing, cottage industries, tailoring and so on. The members generally agreed to divide group loans in rotations on the basis of consumption/business priority without involving themselves in conflicts when all were in need of loans. The decision-making powers rested with the members. The maximum repayment period for the loan was fixed at 12 months. In extreme cases, if the loan was not repaid in the scheduled month, the least interest due was to be paid for that month. Discussions with the members showed that group pressure would be brought, though not amounting to coercion, upon the defaulting members. The interest rate charged did not vary among the groups. Members showed maturity in running the organisation. Though they were entrusted with the power of fixing their own rate of interest, and were aware of using it as a regulatory tool for rationing credit, they did not want to cause much inconvenience to their members by hiking interest rates. The SHGs charged a uniform interest rate of 24 per cent, irrespective of the loan amount. The number of installments for the repayment of the loan were usually fixed by the groups. The repayment of loan started in the month following the loan disbursal.

(b) *Quantum of Internal Lending*

The details of quantum of lending disbursed by the groups is given in Table—5.7.

Table—5.7 Quantum of internal lending as on 30.12.1999

S. No.	Credit range	Urban Area		Rural Area		Total	
		No. of groups (N: 20)	% to total	No. of groups (N: 20)	% to total	No. of groups (N: 40)	% to total
1.	Below Rs. 5,000	1	5	–	–	1	2.50
2.	Rs. 5,001–10,000	1	5	3	15	14	10.00
3.	Rs. 10,001–20,000	5	25	12	60	17	42.50
4.	Rs. 20,001–30,000	4	20	3	15	12	30.00
5.	Rs. 30,001 and above	9	45	2	10	6	15.00
	Total	**20**	**100**	**20**	**100**	**40**	**100.00**

The above Table—5.7 and figure 5.1 reveal that in the case of urban area, five per cent of the groups had lent below Rs. 5,000, another five per cent had lent out between Rs. 5,000 to 10,000. A majority of the groups, i.e. 45 per cent had given above Rs. 30,000 as credit to its members. Twenty-five per cent of the groups, that is, five groups had given financial assistance to its members ranging between Rs. 10,001-20,000, while in the case of the rural area, 15 per cent of the groups had disbursed loans between Rs. 5,001-10,000, 60 per cent for Rs. 10,001-20,000, 15 per cent for Rs. 20,001-30,000 and 10 per cent for above Rs. 30,000. Among the total of 40 groups, a majority of the groups, i.e. 42.5 per cent, had given financial assistance between Rs. 10,001-20,000.

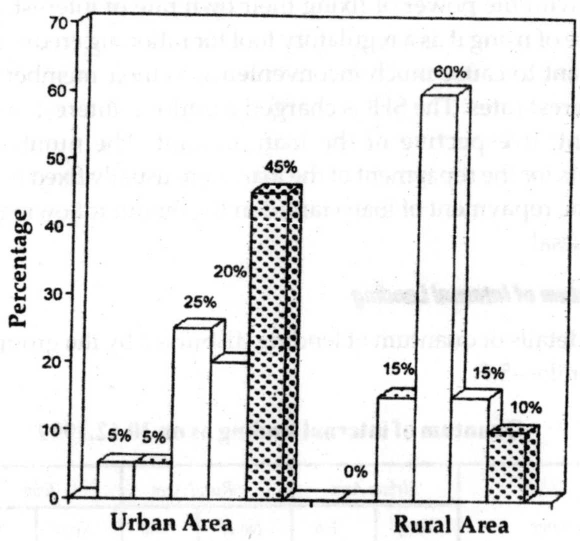

Fig. 5.1: Quantum of Internal Lending upto March 1999

(c) *Purpose of Credit Availed*

Purpose-wise number of SHG members who availed credit from SHG during 1996-99 is given in Table—5.8.

Table—5.8 Purpose-wise number of SHG members who availed credit from SHGs in the study area

S. No.	Purpose	*Urban Area*		*Rural Area*		*Total*	
		No. of members	*% to total*	*No. of members*	*% to total*	*No. of members*	*% to total*
1.	Income generating activities						
	1.1 Agriculture and allied	12	4.29	11	3.65	23	3.96
	1.2 Manufacturing	35	12.50	42	13.95	77	13.25
	1.3 Trading	63	22.50	67	22.26	130	22.37
	1.4 Servicing	11	3.92	13	4.32	24	4.13
	Sub Total	**121**	**43.21**	**133**	**44.18**	**254**	**43.72**
2.	Domestic consumption	67	23.93	95	31.56	162	27.88
3.	Family health	35	12.50	28	9.30	63	10.84
4.	Festivals/ceremonies	20	7.14	12	3.99	32	5.51
5.	Repayment of old debts	25	8.93	15	4.98	40	6.88
6.	Children's education	12	4.29	18	5.98	30	5.16
	Sub Total	**159**	**56.79**	**168**	**55.82**	**327**	**56.28**
	Total	**280**	**100.00**	**301**	**100.00**	**581**	**100.00**

It is seen that 43.72 per cent of SHG members had availed credit for initiating income generating activities. Their proportion in the rural area was 44.18 per cent and in the urban area, 43.21 per cent.

A significant proportion (27.88 per cent) of SHG members availed credit for domestic consumption. Their ratio turned out to be the highest in rural area (31.56 per cent). In the urban area it was (23.93 per cent). Family health (10.84 per cent), repayment of old debts (6.88 per cent), festivals/ceremonies (5.51 per cent) and children's education (5.16 per cent) were other purposes for which SHG members were reported to have availed credit from SHGs. The purpose-wise loans disbursed by SHGs is shown in figure 5.2.

CREDIT FLOW REALISED

The Self Help Credit Management groups are engaged in informal banking operations through the activities of thrift and credit. Tables—5.9 and 5.10 show the details of thrift and credit flow realised, percentage of mean credit to mean thrift, recovery index, outstanding loan for each group in the urban and the rural areas respectively, up to 31st March 1999. A summary of the Table—5.9 and 5.10 is presented in Table—5.11 for an overall position of the groups. The pattern of credit availed by SHG membersin shown in Figure 5.2

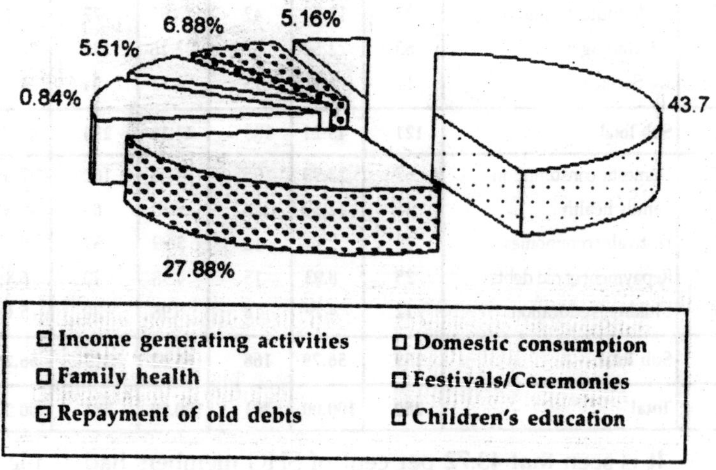

Fig. 5.2: Purpose-wise number of SHG Members who availed Credit from SHG in the Study Area

(a) Thrift Mobilised

In the urban areas, six out of the 20 groups had been in existence for over two years, 12 groups had functioned for over one year and the remaining groups had functioned for less than one year. The amount saved by the individual self-help group was in proportion to the number of months of functioning and the monthly contribution. Totally a sum of Rs. 315300 has been mobilised as savings by 358 members constituting the 20 self help groups in the urban areas. The average savings per member were Rs. 880.73. In fact, high variation in the average savings per member per group can be attributed to the size of SHG.

Table—5.9 Credit flow up to 31st March 1999 (Urban)

S.No.	Name of the groups	No. of members	Age of the group in months	Saving rate per month (Rs.)	Thrift mobilised (Rs.)	Credit disbursed (Rs.)	Mean thrift (Rs.)	Mean credit (Rs.)	% of mean credit to mean thrift	% level of saving	Demand for recovery (Rs.)	Amount recovered (Rs.)	Recovery wise x Rate	Over due (Rs.)	Outstanding loan (Rs.)	% of outstanding to total loan
1	2	3	4	5	6	7	8	9	10	11	12	13	14	15	16	17
1.	C01	20	19	50	19000	46500	950	2325	244.74	100	24450	23650	96.73	800	26000	55.91
2.	C02	15	19	50	14250	34000	950	2267.66	238.60	100	21767	20167	92.65	1600	15600	45.88
3.	C03	16	13	50	10000	9500	625	593.75	95	96	6460	6460	100.00	–	3600	37.89
4.	C04	15	19	50	14250	17000	950	1133.33	119.30	100	15849	14549	91.80	1300	3300	19.41
5.	C05	15	18	50	13500	17000	900	1133.33	125.93	100	9940	9140	91.95	800	8200	48.24
6.	C06	20	12	50	12000	20900	600	1045	174.17	100	12120	12120	100.00	–	11710	56.03
7.	C07	15	23	50	17250	23600	1150	1573.33	136.81	100	17301	17301	100.00	–	9400	39.83
8.	C08	17	13	50	11050	19950	650	1173.53	180.54	100	11810	11810	100.00	–	10850	54.39
9.	C09	15	30	50	22500	48200	1500	3213.33	214.22	100	29550	29550	100.00	–	22250	46.16
10.	C10	20	8	50	8000	10100	400	505.00	126.25	100	2710	2710	100.00	–	7650	75.74
11.	C11	20	32	50	32000	55000	1600	2750	171.88	100	33200	30700	92.47	2500	27300	49.64
12.	C12	20	32	50	32000	55000	1600	2750	171.88	100	28500	26200	91.93	2300	31700	57.64
13.	C13	15	24	50	18000	43000	1200	2866.67	238.89	100	26970	26970	100.00	–	18000	41.86

(Table Contd...)

1	2	3	4	5	6	7	8	9	10	11	12	13	14	15	16	17
14.	C14	20	13	50	13000	24300	650	1215	186.92	100	16343	15123	92.54	1220	10600	43.62
15.	C15	20	11	50	11000	24300	550	1225	222.73	100	16258	14344	88.23	1914	11400	46.53
16.	C16	20	11	50	11000	14500	550	725	131.82	100	11752	4917	41.84	6835	4200	28.97
17.	C17	20	3	50	3000	3000	150	150	100.00	100	260	260	100.00	–	2800	93.33
18.	C18	15	22	50	16500	47700	1100	3180	289.09	100	31530	31530	100.00	–	20400	42.77
19.	C19	20	18	50	18000	45500	900	2275	252.78	100	27404	27404	100.00	–	19450	42.75
20.	C20	20	19	50	19000	53400	950	2670	281.05	100	37045	37045	100.00	–	22800	42.70
	Total	**353**			**3,15,300**	**6,12,650**	**880.73**	**1711.31**	**194.31**	**–**	**3,81,219**	**3,61,950**	**94.95**	**19,269**	**2,87,210**	**46.88**

Table—5.10 Credit flow up to 31st March, 1999 (Rural)

S. No.	Name of the group	No. of members	Age of the group in months	Saving rate per month (Rs.)	Thrift mobilised (Rs.)	Credit disbursed (Rs.)	Mean thrift (Rs.)	Mean credit (Rs.)	% of mean credit to mean thrift	% level of saving	Demand for recovery (Rs.)	Amount recovered (Rs.)	Recovery wise x rate	Over due (Rs.)	Outstanding loan (Rs.)	% of outstanding to total loan
1	2	3	4	5	6	7	8	9	10	11	12	13	14	15	16	17
1.	K01	18	13	50	11,700	25,000	650	1388.89	213.68	100	14,508	14,508	100		11,500	46.00
2.	K02	15	12	50	9,000	12,400	600	826.67	137.78	100	4,750	4,750	100		8,100	65.32
3.	K03	20	16	50	16,000	32,200	800	1610.00	201.25	96	25,700	25,700	100		9,450	29.35
4.	K04	20	15	30	9,000	13,600	450	680.00	151.11	100	10,200	10,200	100		5,300	38.97
5.	K05	16	15	30	7,200	15,000	450	937.50	208.33	100	10,758	8,758	81.41	2000	4,900	32.67
6.	K06	19	15	30	8,550	9,000	450	473.68	105.26	100	5,160	5,160	100		4,100	45.46
7.	K07	19	11	30	6,270	8,500	330	447.37	135.57	100	3,966	3,966	100		4,800	56.47
8.	K08	10	23	30	6,900	11,500	690	1150.00	166.67	100	5,404	5,404	100		6,700	58.26
9.	K09	20	20	30	12,000	16,000	600	800.00	133.33	100	8,400	8,400	100		7,740	48.38
10.	K10	20	24	30	14,400	27,000	720	1350.00	187.50	100	17,660	17,660	100		11,000	40.74
11.	K11	15	19	30	8,400	15,000	560	1000.00	178.57	98.25	13,966	13,966	100		1,900	12.67
12.	K12	15	16	30	7,200	14,500	480	966.67	201.39	100	8,726	8,726	100		6,700	46.21
13.	K13	15	22	30	9,900	13,000	660	866.67	131.31	100	5,508	5,508	100		8,000	61.54
14.	K14	20	22	30	13,200	24,700	660	1235.00	187.12	100	17,790	17,790	100		8,200	33.20

(Table Contd...)

1	2	3	4	5	6	7	8	9	10	11	12	13	14	15	16	17
15.	K15	20	22	30	13,200	30,500	660	1525.00	231.06	100	20,090	20,090	100		12,400	40.66
16.	K16	20	18	30	10,800	15,000	540	750.00	138.89	100	5,610	5,610	100		9,900	66.00
17.	K17	20	15	30	9,000	7,000	450	350.00	77.78	100	3,810	3,810	100		3,500	50.00
18.	K18	20	15	30	9,000	15,000	450	750.00	166.67	100	9,722	9,722	100		9,400	51.09
19.	K19	15	18	30	8,100	15,000	540	1000.00	185.19	100	7,742	7,742	100		7,700	51.33
20.	K20	20	14	50	14,000	16,500	700	825.00	117.86	100	6,318	6,318	100		10,700	64.85
	Total	**357**			**2,03,820**	**3,36,400**	**570.92**	**942.30**	**165.05**	**-**	**2,05,788**	**2,03,788**	**99.03**	**2,000**	**1,47,580**	**43.87**

Table—5.11 Summary of tables 5.9 and 5.10 up to 31.03.1999

S. No.	Details		Urban Area (N : 358)	Rural Area (N : 357)
1.	Total thrift mobilised	Rs.	315300	203820
2.	Total credit disbursed	Rs.	612650	336400
3.	Mean thrift	Rs.	880.73	570.92
4.	Mean credit	Rs.	1711.31	942.30
5.	Percentage of mean credit to mean thrift (Velocity of internal lending)		194.31	165.05
6.	Demand for recovery	Rs.	381219	205788
7.	Amount recovered	Rs.	361950	203788
8.	Recovery index		94.45	99.03
9.	Overdue	Rs.	19269	2000
10.	Outstanding loan	Rs.	287210	147580
11.	Percentage of outstanding to total loan		46.88	43.87

From the details in Table—5.11 the following could be deduced.

The rural groups got established and stabilised later than the urban groups. Out of the 20 groups in existence, 16 had been functioning for over one and half years and the remaining four groups were formed only within the past one year. As a consequence of later formation, the savings realised in the areas was also less compared to those in the urban areas, i.e. Rs. 2,03,820 only were mobilised by 357 members from the 20 self help groups. The average savings per member were Rs. 570.92.

(b) Internal Lending

Internal lending to the tune of Rs. 6,12,650 was reported in the urban areas. In the rural areas the internal lending was proportionately low (i.e.) Rs. 3,36,900. Out of 358 members of SHGs in the urban areas, 280 (78 per cent) had benefitted from internal lending.

In the rural areas, 301 out of the 357 SHG members (84 per cent) had availed loan from their respective groups. It is a very encouraging trend, proving the potentials for self help and mutual group, which are the maxims of any developmental agenda.

(c) Utilisation of Credit

Purpose-wise utilisation of credit taken by SHG members is given in Table—5.12.

Table—5.12 Purpose-wise utilisation of credit by SHGs in the study area

(in Rupees)

S. No.	Purpose of loan utilisation	Urban Area		Rural Area		Total	
		Amount	% to total	Amount	% to total	Amount	% to total
1.	Income generating activities	1,88,000	30.82	1,82,400	54.22	3,71,200	39.11
2.	Domestic consumption	2,21,000	36.07	93,000	27.65	3,14,000	33.09
3.	Family health	87,500	14.28	28,000	8.31	1,15,500	12.17
4.	Festival/ceremonies	57,500	9.39	12,000	3.57	69,500	7.32
5.	Repayment of old debts	25,000	4.08	12,000	3.57	37,000	3.90
6.	Children's education	32,850	5.30	9,000	2.68	41,850	4.41
	Total	**6,12,650**	**100.00**	**3,36,400**	**100.00**	**9,48,550**	**100.00**

The item 'income generating activities' claimed a significant share of credit (39.11 per cent). Loan utilised for domestic consumption purpose was also significant at 33.09 per cent. Family health (12.17 per cent), festival and ceremonies (7.32 per cent), repayment of old debts (3.90 per cent) and children's education (4.41 per cent) were the other purposes for which credit had been utilised by SHG members. A further look into the table reveals that an overwhelming proportion of SHG members from rural areas, 54.22 per cent utilised credit from SHG for business purpose. A significant proportion of SHG borrowing (36.07 per cent) in urban areas had been utilised for domestic consumption. The overall pattern of credit utilisation by SHG members is depicted in Figure 5.3.

(d) Relationship between the Age of SHGs and Savings per Member

The relationship between the age of the SHGs and savings per member is studied by using correlation analysis.

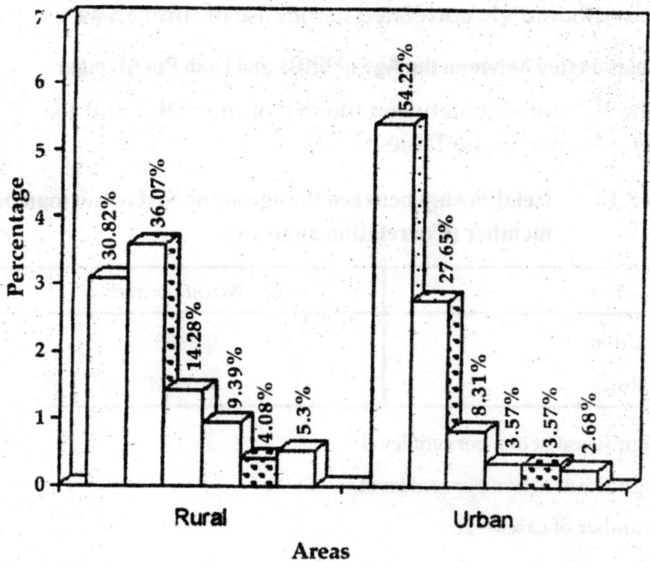

Fig. 5.3: Purpose-wise Utilisation of Credit by SHGs in the Study Area

Table—5.13 Relationship between the age of SHGs and savings per member (Correlation Analysis)

Area	*Co-efficient correlation*
Urban	0.5371**
Rural	0.9999**

** Significant at one per cent level.

Number of cases—20.

The table above shows that the estimation of correlation co-efficient between the age of SHGs and savings per member was statistically significant at one per cent level both in the case of urban areas and in rural areas. The relation between the age of the group and savings per member is highly correlated in the case of urban areas and moderately correlated in the case of rural areas.

(e) Relationship between the Age of SHGs and Loan Per Member

The relationship between the age of the SHGs and loan per member is shown in the Table—5.14.

Table—5.14 Relationship between the age of the SHGs and loan per member (Correlation analysis)

Area	*Co-efficient correlation*
Urban	0.9383**
Rural	0.3128*

** Significant at one per cent level.

* Significant at five per cent level.

Number of cases—20.

The estimation of correlation between the age of SHGs and loan per member was statistically significant at one per cent level in the case of urban groups and five per cent level in the case of rural areas. The relation between the age of the groups and the loan per member is highly correlated in the case of urban areas and moderately correlated in the case of rural areas.

(f) Thrift Credit Ratio

When the thrift credit ratio was calculated, it is found that in the urban areas it was 1: 1.94, which is satisfactory. The corresponding rural figure was 1: 1.65, highlighting the fact that internal lending, which is the crux of SHGs, should be given focal attention in the rural areas.

The details of thrift credit ratio area-wise is presented in Table—5.15.

Table—5.15 Velocity of internal lending

S. No.	Range in percentage	Urban Area		Rural Area	
		No. of groups (N : 20)	Percentage to total	No. of groups (N : 20)	Percentage to total
1.	Below 100	2	10	1	5
2.	101-150	5	25	8	40
3.	Over 150	13	65	11	55
	Total	**20**	**100**	**20**	**100**

From Table—5.15 it was noted that two groups showed the velocity of internal lending to be less than one time (100 per cent), five groups between 1 to 1.5 times (100-150 per cent) and the remaining groups (13) showed the velocity of internal lending to be over 1.5 times (over 150 per cent). Whereas in the case of rural areas, one group showed it to be below 100 percentage of mean credit to mean thrift, eight groups showed between 101 to 150 per cent and 11 groups over 150 per cent.

The 't' value was calculated to find out the difference between the areas in the case of thrift credit ratio.

Table—5.16 Thrift credit ratio

Areas	Number of cases	Mean	Standard deviation
Urban	20	185.13	60.04
Rural	20	162.82	40.24

t value = 1.38

Df = 38

TheTable—5.16 shows that there is no significant difference between the areas regarding the velocity of internal lending of the SHGs.

(g) Recovery Index

The following Table—5.17 gives the picture of recovery index prevailing among the groups.

Table—5.17 Area-wise recovery index

S.No.	Recovery index in percentage	Urban Area		Rural Area		Total	
		No.of groups (N:20)	% to total	No.of groups (N:20)	% to total	No.of groups (N:40)	% to total
1.	Below 80	1	5	–	–	1	2.50
2.	80-90	1	5	1	5	2	5.00
3.	90-99	7	35	–	–	7	17.50
4.	100	11	55	19	95	30	75.00
	Total	**20**	**100.00**	**20**	**100.00**	**40**	**100.00**

It is obvious from the above Table—5.17 that in the case of urban groups, the recovery index was 100 per cent for 11 groups, 90-99 per cent for seven groups, between 80-90 per cent for one group and only one group showed below 80 per cent. As for the rural groups the recovery index was 100 per cent for 19 groups and only one group had a recovery index between 80-90 per cent. The area-wise recovery index is depicted in Figure 5.4.

The overall recovery index for the urban area was 94.95 per cent and the rural area was 99.03 per cent, which are satisfactory levels.

Discussions with the members on the repayment method revealed that in case of delay in deployment of dues by any member, the causes for such default were debated in the meeting and all the groups members, based on merit of the individual, approved necessary postponement of repayment of instalment for that particular month. The members have suggested that the high repayment profile is due to the dynamic incentive system built into the SHGs, under which, groups which had repaid the loan within a stipulated time period were eligible for enhanced loans in the subsequent period. In the sample, a number of SHGs had obtained enhanced loan amount. This dynamic incentive system reinforces the confidence of the members and their continued business relationship with the groups.

(h) Loan Outstanding

The Table—5.18 shows the loan outstanding rate prevailing among the groups, both in the urban and the rural areas and Figure 5.4 shows recovery index area-wise.

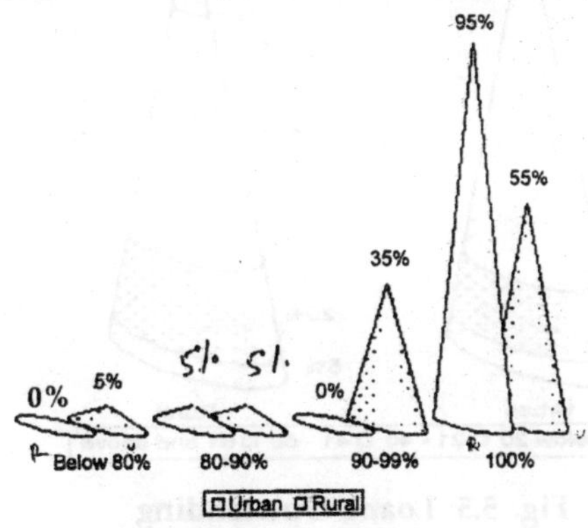

Fig. 5.4: Recovery Index—Area-wise

Table—5.18 Rate of outstanding on total loans

S. No.	Range in percentage	Urban Area		Rural Area	
		No. of groups (N : 20)	Percentage to total	No. of groups (N : 20)	Percentage to total
1.	Below 20	1	5	1	5
2.	21-40	3	15	4	20
3.	41-60	14	70	11	55
4.	61 and above	2	10	4	20
	Total	20	100	20	100

It was noted that more than 61 per cent of the loans were outstanding in two groups in urban areas and four groups in rural areas. In the case of urban areas, 14 groups had 41-60 per cent of loan outstanding, three groups between 21-40 per cent and only one group was below 20 per cent. In the rural areas, 11 groups had loans outstanding between 41-60 per cent, four groups between 21-40 per cent and one group below 20 per cent. The percentage of loan outstanding to total loans is shown in Figure 5.5.

The overall loans outstanding up to March, 1999 was 46.88 per cent in urban areas and 43.87 per cent in rural areas.

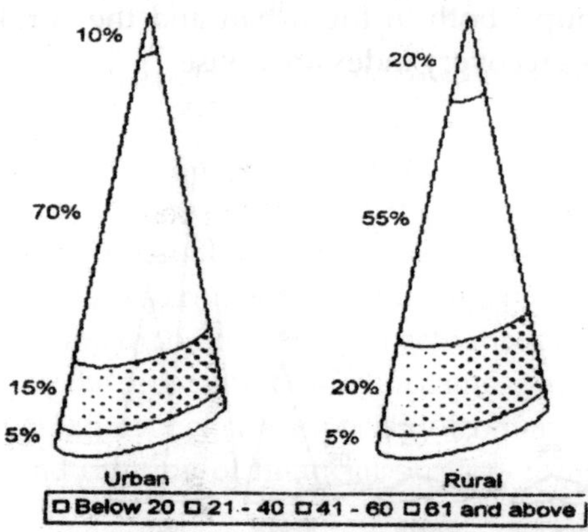

Fig. 5.5: Loans Outstanding

(i) Portfolio—in Arrears Ratio

This is calculated by using the formula.

$$\frac{\text{Payment overdue}}{\text{Payments outstanding}} \times 100$$

Table—5.19 An overall portfolio—in arrears ratio

Area	*Payments overdue (Rs.)*	*Loans outstanding (Rs.)*	*Portfolio in arrears ratio*
Urban	19269	287210	6.71
Rural	2000	147580	1.36

The above Table—5.19 indicates that the portfolio in arrears ratio is 6.71 per cent in the case of urban self help groups, whereas the rural self help groups showed 1.36 per cent. The portfolio in arrears ratio in both the areas was standard as it was less than 10 per cent.

REGRESSION ANALYSIS OF SHGs

In this section an attempt has been made to assess the impact of SHGs on the net income of the SHGs. Accordingly, regression model was specified to find out the major determinants of SHG net income per member. The equation was estimated with qualitative and quantitative variables.

Determinants of SHG Net Income Per Member (Urban Area)

In the regression model (Table—5.20), dependent variable was SHG net income per member, which is defined as interest received + other income minus interest paid + expenditure per member. Explanatory variables were (i) average distance between members in SHGs, (ii) average educational level of members in the SHGs, (iii) loan provided, (iv) age of the SHGs, (v) percentage share of SHGs expenditure in the total income of SHGs.

Table—5.20 Regression estimates: dependent variable SHG net income per member (Urban Area)

Variables	*Co-efficient*	*'t' value*	R^2	*'f' value*
Average distance among members in SHGs	-23.4721	-0.362		
Average education of members in the SHGs	22.7869	-0.543		
Loan provided in the year	0.03506	1.987*	0.6142	3.5028*
Percentage of expenditure in total income	-2.0634	-1.067		
Age of SHGs	2.5341	0.680		

Number of cases–20;

* Significant at five per cent level.

An increase in the average distance among the members in the SHGs leads to decrease of Rs. 23.47 in SHG net income per member. This result is in keeping with the assumption that distance between members of SHG has to be minimal so as to maintain homogeneity and reduce the transaction cost of members, in terms of travelling and opportunity cost of time. The estimate of average educational level of members in the SHGs shows positive contribution to the SHG net income per member. On an average, one year of additional education leads to an increase of Rs. 22.78 per member. Loan provided has contributed to the SHG net income per member positively. One rupee increase in the loan provided to the member results in an increase in SHG net income per member by less than one rupee. An increase in the percentage share of expenditure of SHG in the total income of SHG leads to a decrease in the SHG net income per member by Rs. 2.06. The variables, average distance, average education and percentage of expenditure in total income are not statistically significant. The variable, loan provided in the year, is statistically significant at five per cent level. Age of SHGs positively contributes to the SHGs net income per member. However, this variable is not statistically significant. It is reasonable to expect that the length of the period of existence of SHGs contributes to increase income per member through learning effect. The co-efficient multiple correlation R^2 is 0.6142 showing that 61.42 per cent of variation is explained by the above independent variables. The 'f' value was 3.5028 and it is significant at five per cent level. Therefore, it may be concluded that the selected independent variables were relevant for explaining the variations in SHG net income of the member.

Table—5.21 Regression estimates: dependent variable—SHG net income per member (Rural Area)

Variables	*Co-efficient*	*'t' value*	R^2	*'f' value*
Average distance among members in SHGs	-62.1035	-2.176*		
Average education of members in the SHGs	11.5508	0.821		
Loan provided in the year	0.0674	2.587**	0.6506	4.8406**
Percentage of expenditure in total income	-0.8071	-0.719		
Age of SHGs	3.187	1.610		
Intercept	77.2035	1.559		

* Significant at five per cent level.

** Significant at one per cent level.

Number of cases—20.

From the Table—5.21, it could be observed that an increase in the average distance among the members in the SHGs leads to decrease of Rs. 62.1035 in SHG net income per member which is statistically significant at five per cent level. The estimate of average educational level of members in the SHGs shows positive contribution to the SHG net income per member. On an average, one year of additional education leads to an increase of Rs. 11.55 per member which is not statistically significant. One rupee increase in the loan provided to the member results in an increase in SHG net income per member by less than one rupee. The variable is statistically significant at one per cent level. An increase in the percentage share of expenditure of SHG in the total income of SHG leads to decrease, in the SHG net income per member by Rs. 0.81. However this variable is not statistically significant. Age of SHGs positively contributes to the SHG net income per member and this variable is not statistically significant. The co-efficient multiple correlation R^2 is 0.6506 showing that 65.06 per cent of variation is explained by the above independent variables. The 'f' value was 4.8406 and it is significant at one per cent level. This indicates that the SHG net income per member was influenced by the above mentioned variables.

SUMMARY

The above analysis revealed that the SHGs were able to provide various credit services such as business loan consumption loan, loan for the settlement of old debt and loan for other contingency purposes to their members. The success of SHGs in terms of high repayment is mostly related to the expansion of prevailing social ties and social cohesion found among women members.

6

Impact of Micro Credit on SHG Members

INTRODUCTION

This chapter is mainly devoted to the evaluation of micro-credit assistance to SHG members in quantitative dimensions. For detailed evaluation and analysis, this chapter is divided into four sections. In section I, the socio-economic profile of micro entrepreneurs is presented. Section II describes the economic impact of micro enterprises undertaken by the SHG members in terms of income generation, asset generation, employment generation and the repayment behaviour of the micro entrepreneurs. Section III deals with the social benefits accrued to the members of SHGs and Section IV is an appraisal of the strengths and weaknesses of the SHGs in micro-credit management.

SECTION I

Socio-Economic Profile of Micro Entrepreneurs

The impact of any developmental programme depends upon the socio-economic background of the respondents. The discussion of the socio-economic background of the members has become an integral part of the sociological endeavour. Since the beneficiaries belong mostly to the weaker sections of the society, details of beneficiaries in terms of their social status are provided in this section. The information about socio-economic background of 254 members from the 40 self help groups is provided. A detailed interview schedule was administered to the members to collect the required information.

The socio-economic and demographic details are discussed under the following heads:

(a) Age-wise distribution

(b) Marital status of the respondents

(c) Religion-wise classification

(d) Educational status of the members

(e) Family size

(f) Type of family

(g) Occupational background of the households

(h) Type of house owned by the members

(i) Income level of the households

(a) *Age-wise Distribution*

Age-wise classification of beneficiaries in urban and rural area is given in the Table—6.1.

Table—6.1 Distribution of beneficiaries by the age group—urban and rural areas

Age group	*Urban Area*		*Rural Area*		*Total*	
	No.of beneficiaries	*%of total*	*No.of beneficiaries*	*%of total*	*No.of beneficiaries*	*%of total*
Below 30	17	14.05	17	12.78	34	13.39
31-40	63	52.07	70	52.63	133	52.36
41 and above	41	33.68	46	34.59	87	34.25
Total	**121**	**100.00**	**133**	**100.00**	**254**	**100.00**

The majority of the members, 52.07 per cent in the urban area and 52.63 per cent in the rural area belonged to the age group 31-40 years. Those who were around 30 years constituted 14.05 per cent in the urban area and 12.78 per cent in the rural area. Those who were above 41 years constituted 33.88 per cent and 34.59 per cent in the urban and rural areas respectively. It was interesting to observe that women in the age group of 31-40 years were found in large numbers both in the urban as well as in the rural areas, indicating that women comprehend well the economic necessities and the need to augment the income levels of the families.

(b) *Marital Status of the Respondents*

Information about marital status is shown in Table—6.2.

Table—6.2 Marital status of the beneficiaries in urban and rural areas

Marital status	Urban area		Rural area		Total	
	No. of beneficiaries	% of total	No. of beneficiaries	% of total	No. of beneficiaries	% of total
Married	109	90.08	113	84.96	222	87.40
Un-married	6	4.96	17	12.78	23	9.06
Widow	7	4.96	3	2.26	9	3.54
Total	**121**	**100.00**	**133**	**100.00**	**254**	**100.00**

It could be noted that 90.08 per cent of the beneficiaries in the urban area and 84.96 per cent in the rural area were married. The unmarried constituted 4.96 per cent in the urban area and 12.78 per cent in the rural area. Among the urban group members, 4.96 per cent and among the rural groups 2.26 per cent were widowed.

(c) *Religion-wise Classification*

Classification of the members on the basis of religion is shown in Table—6.3.

Table—6.3 Religion-wise classification of beneficiaries in the urban and rural areas

Religion	Urban area		Rural area		Total	
	No. of beneficiaries	% of total	No. of beneficiaries	% of total	No. of beneficiaries	% of total
Hindu	99	81.82	108	81.20	207	81.50
Muslim	12	9.92	10	7.52	22	8.66
Christian	10	8.26	15	11.28	25	9.84
Total	**133**	**100.00**	**121**	**100.00**	**254**	**100.00**

Information reported in Table—6.3 indicated that predominantly the members were Hindus (81.82 per cent) and (81.20 per cent), followed by Muslims (9.92 per cent) and (7.52 per cent) and Christians (8.26 per cent) and (11.28 per cent) in both urban and rural areas respectively.

(d) *Educational Status of the Members*

A minimum level of education is absolutely essential for the active participation of women in the development programme. In fact, education is one of the most essential inputs of the rural development process. It has been found that there is a high degree of correlation between the level of education and productivity among the women. For adoption of new techniques of production, women must be educated. Education can remove ignorance, superstition and disinclination to accept change. Hence details relating to the educational status of the beneficiaries are presented in Table—6.4.

Table—6.4 Educational status of the beneficiaries in the urban and rural areas

Level of education	*Urban area*		*Rural area*		*Total*	
	No. of beneficiaries	*% of total*	*No. of beneficiaries*	*% of total*	*No. of beneficiaries*	*% of total*
Illiterate	13	10.74	15	11.28	28	11.02
Below primary	17	14.05	11	8.27	28	11.02
Primary school	37	30.58	39	29.32	76	29.92
Middle school	25	20.66	37	27.82	62	24.41
Secondary school	24	19.83	21	15.79	45	17.72
Higher secondary school	4	3.31	8	6.02	12	4.72
College/University	1	0.83	2	1.50	3	1.18
Total	121	100.00	133	100.00	254	100.00

In the case of the urban area, out of 121 women, 13 women (10.74 per cent) were totally illiterate. It might be noted that 14.05 per cent had the ability just to read and write, 30.58 per cent received primary education, 20.66 per cent had studied up middle school level, 19.83 per cent had secondary education, 3.31 per cent had higher secondary education and 0.83 per cent college/university education. While in the case of the rural area, illiterates constituted 11.28 per cent, 8.27 per cent of them were educated below primary level, 27.82 per cent of them were educated up to middle school, followed by primary 29.32 per cent, secondary level 15.79 per cent, higher secondary level 6.02 per cent and higher education level 1.50 per cent.

Since most of the respondents had studied only upto middle school level, they could not take up any other form of employment requiring high skill and formal education. So they were motivated to join the self help group and start micro enterprises.

(e) *Family Size*

The distribution of beneficiary families according to the family size has been presented in Table—6.5.

Table—6.5 Distribution of beneficiaries in urban and rural area by family size

	Urban area		*Rural area*		*Total*	
Size of the family	*No. of beneficiaries*	*% of total*	*No. of beneficiaries*	*% of total*	*No. of beneficiaries*	*% of total*
1 to 4 members	80	66.12	102	76.69	182	71.65
5 and above	41	33.88	31	23.31	72	28.35
Total	**121**	**100.00**	**133**	**100.00**	**254**	**100.00**

It can be seen that 66.12 per cent of the families in the urban area and 76.69 per cent of the families in the rural area had around four members. The percentages of rural and urban area families having more than four members per family, was 23 31 and 33.38 respectively. It confirms the observation that the urban slums tend to have large number of family members, compared to rural areas. These urban families do not have much access to information on small family norm nor the awareness about limiting family size, owing to illiteracy and indifference regarding family size.

It was observed from the above table that out of 254 beneficiaries, 182 (71.65 per cent) beneficiary, families had four members and the remaining (28.35 per cent) had a family of five members.

(f) *Type of family*

The type of family of the beneficiaries in the urban and rural area is discussed in the Table--6.6.

Table—6.6 Family type of the beneficiaries in the urban and rural areas

Type	Urban area		Rural area		Total	
	No. of beneficiaries	% of total	No. of beneficiaries	% of total	No. of beneficiaries	% of total
Nuclear family	87	71.90	102	76.69	189	74.41
Joint family	34	28.10	31	23.31	65	25.59
Total	**121**	**100.00**	**133**	**100.00**	**254**	**100.00**

It was observed that 71.90 per cent of the beneficiaries in the urban area and 77 per cent of the beneficiaries in the rural area belonged to nuclear family. In the case of joint families 28 per cent of the beneficiaries were from urban area and 23.31 per cent were from rural areas. On the whole, the nuclear family system was predominant among the entire sample studied.

(g) *Occupational Background of the Households*

Table—6.7 gives the distribution of self-help group members by the main occupation of the head of the household.

Table—6.7 Distribution of beneficiaries in urban and rural areas by main occupation

Main occupation	Urban area		Rural area		Total	
	No. of beneficiaries	% of total	No. of beneficiaries	% of total	No. of beneficiaries	% of total
Salaried work	5	4.13	6	4.51	11	4.33
Casual labour (including agri-cultural labour)	37	30.58	58	43.61	95	37.40
Petty business	48	39.67	39	29.32	87	34.25
Artisans	31	25.62	30	22.58	61	24.02
Total	**121**	**100.00**	**133**	**100.00**	**254**	**100.00**

The major item of occupation observed among the SHG members was casual labour (37.40 per cent). This is more evident in rural (43.61 per cent) as compared to urban areas (30.58 per cent). Salaried workers (4.13 per cent), artisans (25.62 per cent) and petty businessmen (39.67 per cent) was the next significant occupation group in the urban area. Artisans constituted 22.58 per cent, salaried workers 4.51 per cent and those who pursued petty business constituted 29.32 per cent in the rural area.

(h) *Type of House Owned by the Members*

A house, no doubt, provides shelter, but its type indicates the economic and social status of beneficiaries. The poverty levels are replaced by the type of house owned by families. It may be observed from Table—6.8 that 27.3 per cent of the beneficiaries in the urban area and 20.3 per cent of the beneficiaries in the rural area own houses which may be considered as pucca (tiled house).

Table—6.8 Classification of beneficiaries as per type of house

Type of house	*Urban area*		*Rural area*		*Total*	
	No. of beneficiaries	*% of total*	*No. of beneficiaries*	*% of total*	*No. of beneficiaries*	*% of total*
Hut	3	2.48	15	11.28	19	7.09
Kutcha	8	6.61	39	29.32	48	18.50
Semi-pucca (semi tiled)	76	62.81	46	34.59	122	48.03
Pucca (tiled)	33	27.27	27	20.30	60	23.62
Rented	1	0.83	6	4.51	7	2.76
Total	121	100.00	133	100.00	254	100.00

By personal observation, the researcher had found that even the so-called pucca houses did not provide enough accommodation to all the family members. They are pucca in the sense that they do not collapse to the furies of nature. Kutcha house and hut dwellers accounted for nearly nine per cent in the case of urban families and nearly four per cent in case of rural families. Chi-square test revealed that there is a significant difference in the type of house between the urban and the rural areas.

(i) *Income Level of the Households*

The members were classified into five categories on the basis of their annual income in the base year. The classification is presented in Table—6.9.

Table—6.9 Income levels of the members in urban and rural areas

Range of income (Rs.)	Urban area		Rural area		Total	
	No. of beneficiaries	% of total	No. of beneficiaries	% of total	No. of beneficiaries	% of total
Below 5,000	39	32.24	43	32.33	82	32.28
5,001-10,000	64	52.89	61	45.87	125	49.22
10,001-11,500	2	1.65	4	3.01	6	2.36
11,501-13,600	5	4.13	7	5.26	12	4.72
13,600 and above	11	9.09	18	13.53	29	11.42
Total	**121**	**100.00**	**133**	**100.00**	**254**	**100.00**

A look into the data reveals that out of 121 members in the urban slum area 11 members (9.09 per cent) had an income over Rs. 13,600 per annum, five members (4.13 per cent) were earning more than Rs. 11,500 but less than Rs. 13,600 per annum, two members (1.65 per cent) were earning between Rs. 10,001-11,500 per annum, 64 members (52.89 per cent) and 39 members (32.24 per cent) had an annual income between Rs. 5,001 to Rs. 10,000 and less than Rs. 5,000 respectively.

A similar trend could be observed in the case of rural area. A majority of the members (45.87 per cent) were in the category of Rs. 5,001-10,000 per annum and 32.33 per cent of the were members in the category of below Rs. 5,000 per annum. The table also shows that 18 members (13.53 per cent) were earning an annual income in over Rs. 13,600. Out of 254 members, 29 members (11.42 per cent) belonged to the highest income group of Rs. 13,600 and above per annum.

SECTION II

Economic Returns from the Micro Enterprises Undertaken

In this section, the economic returns from the micro enterprises initiated by the SHG women was analysed in detail. The economic impact was measured on the basis of the increase in income due to the financial assistance given to each member. The assistance was given to the micro entrepreneurs to acquire a productive asset which creates adequate employment and thereby, generate the required income to enable the family to cross the poverty line. But when assistance is given to the poorest of the poor on need basis, there may be improvement in the family income, but those families may not be able to cross the poverty line. Thus when families in a lower income group move into a higher income group, the impact is said to be favourable. Such upward shift of families from lower income to higher income groups is also presented in this section. Further, an attempt is also made in this section to assess the impact of various enterprises on generation of additional employment in the enterprises.

The following headings give information on:

(a) Sources of indebtedness

(b) Investment pattern

(c) Income generation

(d) Asset generation

(e) Employment generation

(f) Recovery performance

(a) *Sources of Indebtedness*

The extent of indebtedness of micro entrepreneurs of the SHGs according to sources and the amount of debt are given in Table—6.10.

It could be seen that the banks provided 45.97 per cent of loan amount to the members. As high as 35.29 per cent of the loan amount was borrowed from their own SHGs. Corpus fund of Avinashilingam Education Trust Institution emerged as the third prominent source of lending (8.36 per cent) to SHG members. Friends and relatives (6.89 per cent) and moneylenders (3.49 per cent) also provided credit to micro entrepreneurs. It was also noted that the loan borrowed from SHGs was the highest (76.52 per cent) in the case of rural areas and the amount borrowed from banks was the highest (58.51 per cent) in the case of urban areas, because access to the banks among urban women was easier compared to that among rural women.

Table—6.10 Extent of indebtedness of SHG members according to sources and amount of debt

(in Rupees)

Sources	Amount borrowed		
	Urban	*Rural*	*Total*
SHGs	1,88,800 (28.62)	1,82,400 (76.52)	3,71,200 (35.29)
Scheduled Banks	3,86,000 (58.51)	97,500 (24.86)	4,83,500 (45.97)
Friends and relatives	27,000 (4.09)	45,500 (11.60)	72,500 (6.89)
Money lenders	–	36,750 (9.37)	36,750 (3.49)
Corpus fund (Avinashilingam Education Trust institution)	57,900 (8.78)	30,000 (7.60)	87,900 (8.36)
Total	**6,59,700 (100.00)**	**3,92,150 (100.00)**	**10,51,850 (100.00)**

(Figures in parentheses indicate percentage to column total).

(b) *Investment Pattern*

As revealed in Table—6.11 amount of investments made in micro projects by entrepreneurs across the study areas ranged from less than Rs. 1,000 to more than Rs. 10,000 (Figure 6.1).

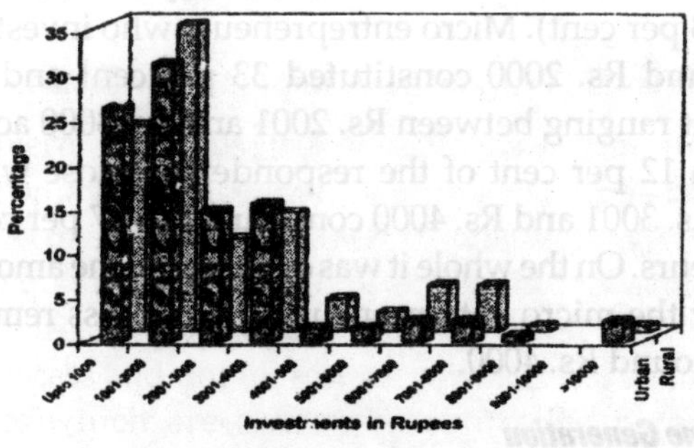

Fig. 6.1: Investment Pattern in Micro Projects by Entrepreneurs of SHGs

Table—6.11 Investment pattern in micro projects by entrepreneurs of SHGs

(in Rupees)

Investment	*Urban area*		*Rural area*		*Total*	
	Number of members	*Percentage*	*Number of members*	*Percentage*	*Number of members*	*Percentage*
Upto 1000	32	26.45	31	23.31	63	24.80
1001-2000	38	31.40	46	34.58	84	33.07
2001-3000	18	14.88	14	10.53	32	12.60
3001-4000	19	15.70	18	13.54	37	14.57
4001-5000	2	1.65	5	3.76	37	2.76
5001-6000	2	1.65	3	2.26	5	1.97
6001-7000	3	2.48	7	5.26	10	3.94
7001-8000	3	2.48	7	5.26	10	3.94
8001-9000	1	0.83	1	0.75	2	0.79
9001-10000	–	–	–	–	–	–
> 10000	3	2.48	1	0.75	4	1.56
Total	**121**	**100.00**	**133**	**100.00**	**254**	**100.00**

It could be noted that, on the whole 1.56 per cent of entrepreneurs have invested more than Rs. 10,000. This proportion was comparatively more in urban areas (2.48 per cent). On the contrary, micro entrepreneurs who invested less than Rs. 1000 were more prominent both in the urban (26.45 per cent) and the rural areas (23.3 per cent). Micro entrepreneurs who invested between Rs. 1001 and Rs. 2000 constituted 33 per cent and those with investment ranging between Rs. 2001 and Rs. 3000 accounted for more than 12 per cent of the respondents. Those who invested between Rs. 3001 and Rs. 4000 constituted 14.57 per cent of micro entrepreneurs. On the whole it was evident that the amount of credit needed by the micro entrepreneurs more or less remained at an amount around Rs. 4000.

(c) *Income Generation*

The data relating to the average household income of the members was estimated at two points of time i.e., base year and post-credit year. Since the members were assisted in the year

1996-97, the income in that year was taken as the base year income. A two year gap was given for the financial assistance to produce the necessary impact on the level of income. Data on household income was therefore, collected in the year 1999-2000. Impact on income generation was studied both area-wise and sector/ enterprise-wise under the following subheadings:

(i) Increase in income

(ii) Investment-income ratio in micro enterprises of SHGs

(iii) Relationship between investment and income of the micro entrepreneurs—correlation analysis

(iv) Shift of the households above poverty line

(v) Shift of beneficiaries to higher income groups

(vi) Sources of credit and the determinants influencing household income of the members—regression analysis

(i) Increase in Income

Area-wise Increase in Income

The data relating to the household income earned by the members—area-wise in the base and post credit years are presented in Table—6.12. It can be observed from the table that the average income in all the areas had increased in the year 1999-2000 compared to that of the base year.

Area-wise incremental income analysis was made because the abilities of the entrepreneurs to manage project normally vary with the geographical location of the family. An attempt was made to find out whether the area had any role in determining the increase in income. The increase in income of the micro entrepreneurs area-wise is shown in the Table—6.12. It is evident that the incremental income of the members in urban area was Rs. 4964.53 and rural area was Rs. 4095.34. The percentage variation in income of all the 254 households was 53.62 per cent, while that of 121 urban households was 62.79 per cent. The average income of 133 households belonging to rural area was higher both in the base year and the post-project year. It means that the rural households are better off compared to urban households as both the points of time. The calculated 't' values between the pre- and post-credit

Table—6.12 Area-wise average household income of the micro entrepreneurs in the base year and post-credit year

(in rupees)

S. No.	*Area*	*Average net income*				*Incremental income*	*SD*	*Percentage variation*	*Paired 't' value*
		Base year	*SD*	*Post project year*	*SD*				
1.	Urban	7907.04	5966.58	12871.57	7660.81	4964.53	3776.92	62.79	14.46**
2.	Rural	8866.32	5090.15	12961.65	6901.69	4095.34	3887.05	46.19	12.15**
	Total	**8409.34**	**5534.79**	**12918.74**	**7258.81**	**4509.40**	**3852.05**	**53.62**	**18.66****

programme, incomes of the beneficaries belonging to different areas are statistically significant.

Enterprise-wise Increase in Income

The data relating to the average income by enterprises in the base year and post credit years are presented in Table—6.13 and Figure 6.2. Needless to say that the income generating capacity of different entrepreneurs will be different. It can be observed from the Table—6.12 that the average net income in all the entrepreneurs has increased in the year 1999-2000 compared to that in the base year.

The average household income of the members, which was Rs. 8,409.34 prior to micro credit assistance, increased to Rs. 12,918.74. The average increase in household income of the members worked out to be Rs. 4,509.40 which represents 53.62 per cent. In the agricultural and allied sector, the average household annual income of 23 micro entrepreneurs increased from Rs. 9,239.13 to Rs. 13,111.74 showing an increase of Rs. 3,872.61 (41.92 per cent). The incremental income of Rs. 5,393.91 indicating an increase of 81.45 per cent in the cottage industries was the highest compared to all the other entrepreneurs in all the three sectors. In the agriculture sector, the incremental income of Rs. 4,410.00 in the dairy farming was the highest compared to other enterprises. The calculated 't' values between the pre- and post-credit period, income of the beneficiaries belonging to different enterprises are statistically significant.

(ii) Investment-Income Ratio in Macro Enterprises of SHGs

Investment-Income Ratio—Area-wise

Table—6.14 shows the area-wise ratio of income to investment.

The net income generated from the micro enterprises of both urban slum and rural area are presented in the Table—6.14. It can be observed from the table that among the areas urban entrepreneurs have generated the highest income with an investment income ratio of 1.039 (103.97 per cent). The rural entrepreneurs have generated 60.86 per cent. It can also be seen that the average net income from all the areas was Rs. 4191.46, which flowed from an average investment of Rs. 5358.38 giving an investment income ratio of 0.78 (78.22 per cent).

Table—6.13 Average net household income of the micro entrepreneurs of SHGs in the base year and post credit year

(Sector Micro Enterprise-wise)

S. No.	Sector/Micro enterprises	Base year		Post credit year		Percentage increase		Percentage variation	Paired 't' value
		Mean income	Standard deviation	Mean income	Standard deviation	Mean income	Standard deviation		
I.	**Agriculture**	9239.13		13111.74		3872.61		41.92	
	1. Dairy farming	10060.00	5045.83	14470.00	5667.26	4410.00	2079.24	43.84	6.71**
	2. Poultry	7175.00	2338.34	10458.75	3387.99	3283.75	3161.12	45.77	2.94*
	3. Sheep and goat rearing	10900.00	7567.69	14640.00	9484.09	3740.00	2599.62	34.31	3.22*
II.	**Manufacturing**	8197.71		13282.98		5085.27		62.03	
	1. Cottage industries	7236.52	4518.50	13130.43	6574.78	5893.91	3783.69	81.45	7.47**
	2. Detergent making	9349.20	10909.87	13337.00	11871.48	3987.80	4006.75	42.65	4.45**
	3. Food processing/catering	8170.59	4194.70	13354.41	6466.98	5183.82	4068.44	63.44	7.43**
III.	**Trading**	8306.21		12572.08		4265.87		51.36	
	1. Petty shops	8353.51	4381.67	13461.89	7787.12	5108.38	5365.34	61.15	5.79**
	2. Sale of cloth	8200.61	4377.94	12599.57	6626.10	4398.96	3853.67	53.64	7.74**
	3. Sale of food items (Vegetable and fruits)	8372.34	5473.36	11844.68	5924.55	3472.34	2451.95	41.47	9.71**
IV.	**Servicing**	8851.67		13442.91		4591.24		51.87	
	1. Tailoring	9527.27	7377.95	14436.36	9607.42	4909.09	4327.92	51.53	3.76**
	2. Grinding	10400.00	7257.55	15638.33	10632.44	5238.33	4905.10	50.37	2.62**
	3. Laundry	6462.86	2277.06	10000.00	2364.32	3537.14	1095.59	54.73	8.54**
	Total	**8409.34**	**5534.79**	**12918.74**	**7258.81**	**4509.40**	**3852.05**	**53.62**	**18.66****

Note: ** Significant at one per cent level.

* Significant at 5 per cent level.

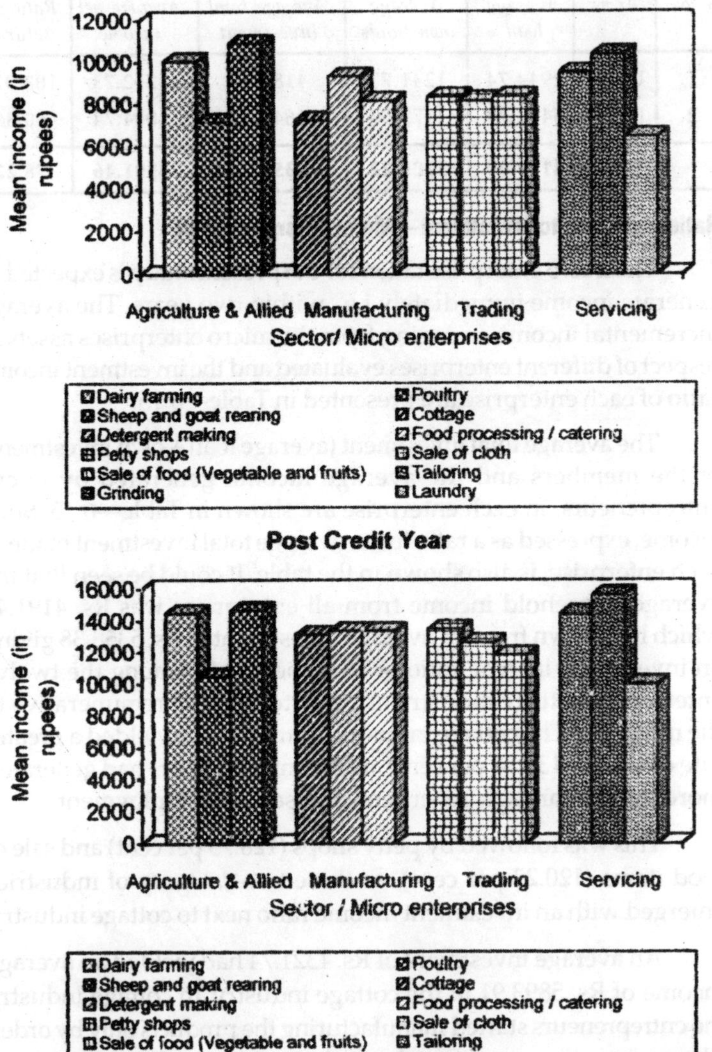

Fig. 6.2: Average Net Household Income of the Micro Entrepreneurs of SHGs in the Base Year and Post-Credit Year

Table—6.14 Ratio of income to investment—Area-wise

(in Rupees)

S. No.	Areas	Average loan	Average own funds	Average total investment	Average net income	Ratio of return
1.	Urban	2944.74	1241.73	4186.47	4352.73	103.97
2.	Rural	5472.73	1173.50	6646.23	4044.74	60.86
	Total	**4149.00**	**1209.22**	**5358.38**	**4191.46**	**78.22**

Ratio of Income to Investment—Micro Enterprise-wise

The micro enterprise taken for the present study is expected to generate income immediately i.e., within two years. The average incremental income emerging from the micro enterprises assets in respect of different enterprises evaluated and the investment income ratio of each enterprise are presented in Table—6.15.

The average total investment (average loan + own investment) of the members and the average income generated by micro entrepreneurs, in each enterprise are shown in Table—6.15. Such income, expressed as a ratio to the average total investment made in each enterprise, is also shown in the table. It could be seen that the average household income from all enterprises was Rs. 4191.46 which had flown from an average investment of Rs. 5358.38 giving an investment income ratio of 78.22 per cent. Among the twelve enterprises, cottage industry appears to be more remunerative to the members. The cottage industry seems to have yielded a greater rate of return (136.38 per cent), as the entrepreneurs had generated more income through generation of assets and employment.

This was followed by petty shops (128.75 per cent) and sale of food items (120.23 per cent), as these two category of industries emerged with an investment income ratio next to cottage industry.

An average investment of Rs. 4321.74 had yielded an average income of Rs. 5893.91 in the cottage industry. In cottage industry the entrepreneurs started manufacturing the products only by order. There was no surplus of goods in hand. Whatever they manufactured, they sold immediately. Petty shop enterprises had also yielded a high rate of return, as their customers were frequent buyers. Moreover, these entrepreneurs sold a variety of goods which were in demand in the local area and they kept changing the products according to the requirements of the customers. Sale of food items (vegetable and fruit vending) enterprise had also yielded a rate of return of 120.23 per cent, which was more than the average rate of return of 78.22 per cent from all enterprises. In the detergent-making trade, the rate of return appeared to be very less (21.31 per cent), because some of the entrepreneurs used the loan, not for investment purpose, but for repayment of previous loans.

Table—6.15 Ratio of income to investment (Micro-enterprise-wise)

(in rupees)

S. No.	Sectors/Micro enterprises	Average loan	Average own funds	Average total investment	Average net income	Rate of return (%)
I.	**Agriculture**	**2191.30**	**1983.91**	**4175.21**	**3872.61**	**92.75**
	1. Dairy farming	2000.00	2205.00	4205.00	4410.00	104.88
	2. Poultry	1862.50	1125.00	2987.50	3283.75	109.92
	3. Sheep and goat rearing	3100.00	2916.00	6016.00	3740.00	62.17
II.	**Manufacturing**	**7072.73**	**1297.05**	**8369.78**	**5085.27**	**60.76**
	1. Cottage industry	3363.04	958.70	4321.74	5893.91	136.38
	2. Detergent making	16940.00	1769.40	18709.40	3987.80	21.31
	3. Food processing/ catering	3777.94	1248.08	5026.02	5183.82	103.14
III.	**Trading**	**3005.00**	**906.92**	**3911.92**	**4265.89**	**109.05**
	1. Petty shop	2925.68	1042.30	3967.98	5108.38	128.75
	2. Sale of cloth	4003.26	909.79	4913.05	4398.96	89.54
	3. Sale of food items (vegetables, fruits)	2090.43	797.55	2887.98	3472.34	120.23
IV.	**Servicing**	**2841.67**	**1822.50**	**4664.17**	**4591.24**	**98.44**
	1. Tailoring	2909.09	2061.82	4970.91	4909.09	98.76
	2. Grinding	3250.00	1500.00	4750.00	5238.33	113.28
	3. Laundry	2385.71	1722.86	4108.57	3537.14	86.09
	Total	**4149.00**	**1209.22**	**5358.38**	**4191.46**	**78.22**

ANOVA test was applied to find out if there was any significant difference between the groups in their average return on investment (Table—6.16).

Table—6.16 Average return on investment among different sectors—ANOVA

Source	*DF*	*Sum of squares*	*Mean squares*	*'t' value*
Between the groups	3	34724.20	11574.73	0.6085
Within the groups	250	4755318.46	19021.27	
Total	**253**	**4790042.66**		

The calculated 't' value was not significant, so there is no significant difference in the average return on investment of the different groups. This means that the groups do not differ significantly in their average return on investment.

(iii) Relationship between Investment and Average Household Income of the Micro Entrepreneurs—Correlation Analysis

Correlation analysis is used to find out the extent of relationship between the investment and household income of the micro entrepreneurs.

Table—6.17 Investment-income relationship—Area-wise (Correlationanalysis)

Area	*Co-efficient correlation*
Urban	0.6207**
Rural	0.2444**

Correlation analysis explains that correlation in both the areas are significant at one per cent level (Table—6.17). Therefore, there is significant positive relationship between the investment and income of the micro entrepreneurs under the micro credit programme in both the areas.

Table—6.18 Investment-income relationship—sector-wise (Correlation analysis)

Sector	*Co-efficient correlation*
Agriculture and allied	0.7820**
Manufacturing	0.6880**
Trading	0.2693**
Servicing	0.6475**

The Table—6.18 reveals that correlation is significant at one per cent level in all the sectors. It could be observed that the co-efficient correlation in the agriculture and allied sector is highly correlated, followed by manufacturing servicing and trading sectors. The correlation in the trading sector is moderately correlated, whereas the correlation between investment and income in the manufacturing and servicing sectors is high. Therefore, there is significant positive relationship between the investment and income of the members under micro credit programme of the SHGs members.

Correlation analysis (Table—6.19) explains that correlation is significant at one per cent level in the case of sheep rearing, detergent making, food processing, sale of cloth and tailoring. The correlation is significant at five per cent level in the case of dairy farming, whereas the correlation is not significant in other enterprises. Therefore, there is positive relationship between investment and income of the entrepreneurs in the case of all the micro enterprises except the petty shop and laundry business.

Table—6.19 Investment-income relationship—micro enterprise-wise (Correlation analysis)

Micro enterprises	*Co-efficient correlation*
1	2
Dairy farming	0.6767*
Poultry	0.1040
Sheep rearing	0.9781**
Cottage industries	0.3360
Detergent making	0.9258**

(Table Contd...)

1	2
Food processing/catering	0.4735**
Petty shop	-0.0497
Sale of cloth	0.4800**
Sale of food items	0.0701
Tailoring	0.8842**
Grinding	0.6596
Laundry	-0.0295

* Significant at five per cent level.

(iv) Shift of the Households above Poverty Line

Micro enterprises are an important source of income and employment generation for a significant section of the poor. In fact, this sub-sector is perceived to be an essential part of survival strategy of poor households. According to 1991 census, micro enterprises sub-sector accounts for 16 per cent of employment of all the main workers. The growth prospects for this sub-sector are more promising. The relationship between micro enterprises and poverty reduction is under serious consideration among the policy-makers and development programme implementers. While a large proportion of the poor still relied on livelihood enterprises for subsistence, some demonstrated their real entrepreneurial potential to lift themselves out of poverty as well as to provide employment to others. Many observers have been emphasising that the micro enterprise sector is an important element in any future strategy for poverty eradication.

The base year for the present study is 1997-98 which falls in the ninth plan period* as per the 9th plan, a person is below the poverty line when his annual income is less than Rs. 15840 for urban areas and Rs. 13680 for rural areas.

The present study estimates the number of households which have crossed the poverty line area-wise and micro enterprise-wise. In estimating such a number, care should be taken to see that the households which were above the poverty line even in the base

* Narasaiah and Reddy, *"The Concept of Poverty, Rhetoric and Reality"*, *Southern Economist*, Vol. 37, No. 17, Jan. 1999, pp. 5-6.

year are eliminated, because the micro credit is introduced for the poorest of the poor households. Such households may move on the income ladder to a higher rung but may not cross the poverty line.

The number of entrepreneurs area-wise crossing the poverty line is presented in Table—6.20.

Table—6.20 Number of entrepreneurs below and above poverty line

S. No	Area	Number of members	Base year poverty line		Post credit year poverty line		Net number crossing poverty line
			Below	Above	Below	Above	
1.	Urban	121 (100.00)	114 (94.21)	7 (5.79)	92 (76.03)	29 (23.97)	22 (18.18)
2.	Rural	133 (100.00)	115 (86.47)	18 (13.53)	98 (73.68)	35 (26.32)	17 (12.78)
	Total	**254 (100.00)**	**229 (90.16)**	**25 (9.84)**	**190 (74.80)**	**64 (25.20)**	**39 (15.36)**

Note: Figure in brackets denotes percentage to total.

It was observed that out of 254 micro entrepreneurs, 25 (9.84 per cent) entrepreneurs were above the poverty line, even in the base year. On the whole, the net number of households crossing the poverty line was 39 (15.36 per cent). Out of 121 micro entrepreneurs of urban slum groups, 29 members (23.97 per cent) had crossed the poverty line, i.e. they crossed the annual income of Rs. 15,840 and the net number of members crossing the poverty line was 22 (18.18 per cent). In the case of rural area, 35 members crossed the poverty line, i.e. they crossed the annual income of Rs. 13,680 and the net number of members crossing the poverty line was 17 (12.78 per cent) (Figure 6.3).

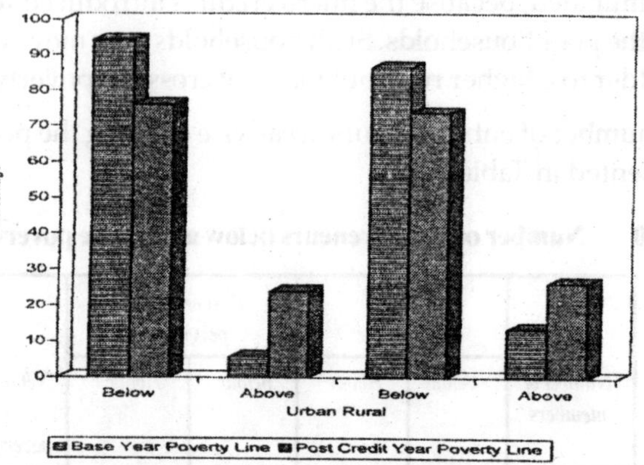

Fig. 6.3: Number of Entrepreneurs below and above Poverty Line

Enterprise-wise Micro Entrepreneurs Crossing the Poverty Line

Enterprise-wise micro entrepreneurs crossing the poverty line is shown in Table—6.21.

Table—6.21 Micro entrepreneurs crossing poverty line—Enterprises-wise

S. No.	Sector/Micro enterprises	Number of members	Base year poverty line		Post credit year poverty line		Net number crossing poverty line
			Below	Above	Below	Above	
1	2	3	4	5	6	7	8
I.	**Agriculture and allied**	23 (100.00)	19 (82.61)	4 (17.39)	16 (69.57)	7 (30.43)	3 (13.00)
	1. Dairy farming	10	7 (70.00)	3 (30.00)	6 (60.00)	4 (40.00)	1 (10.00)
	2. Poultry	8	8 (100.00)	–	7 (87.50)	1 (12.50)	1 (12.50)
	3. Sheep and goat rearing	5	73 (94.81)	1 (20.00)	3 (60.00)	2 (40.00)	1 (20.00)
II.	**Manufacturing**	77 (100.00)	22 (95.65)	4 (5.19)	55 (71.43)	22 (28.57)	18 (23.38)
	1. Cottage industries	23	19 (95.00)	1 (4.35)	17 (73.91)	6 (26.09)	5 (21.74)

(Table Contd...)

1	2	3	4	5	6	7	8
	2. Detergent making	20	32 (94.12)	1 (5.00)	16 (80.00)	4 (20.00)	3 (15.00)
	3. Food processing/ catering	34	117 (90.00)	2 (5.88)	22 (64.71)	12 (35.29)	10 (29.41)
III.	Trading	130 (100.00)	34 (91.89)	13 (10.00)	100 (76.92)	30 (23.08)	17 (13.08)
	1. Petty shop	37	40 (86.96)	3 (8.11)	29 (78.38)	8 (21.62)	5 (13.51)
	2. Sale of cloth	46	43 (91.49)	6 (13.04)	33 (71.74)	13 (28.26)	7 (15.22)
	3. Sale of food items	47	20 (83.33)	4 (8.51)	30 (80.85)	9 (19.15)	5 (10.64)
IV.	Servicing	24 (100.00)	8 (72.73)	4 (16.67)	19 (79.17)	5 (20.83)	1 (4.17)
	1. Tailoring	11	5 (83.33)	3 (27.27)	7 (63.64)	4 (36.36)	1 (16.67)
	2. Grinding	6	7	1 (16.67)	5 (83.33)	1 (16.67)	–
	3. Laundry	7		–	7	–	–
	Total	**254 (100.00)**	**229 (90.16)**	**25 (9.84)**	**190 (74.80)**	**64 (25.20)**	**39 (15.36)**

Note: Figures in brackets denotes percentage to total.

It can be seen from Table—6.21 that out of 254 members, 25 members were above the poverty line even in the base year. On the whole, out of 229 members, 39 members (15.36 per cent) crossed the poverty line. The percentage of poor households crossing the poverty line was 30.43 per cent in the agricultural sector, 28.57 per cent in manufacturing sector, 23.08 per cent in trading sector and 20.83 per cent in servicing sector. The highest percentage of households, which have crossed the poverty line, was in the dairy farming and sheep rearing (40 per cent). Next to these enterprises, food processing in the manufacturing sector and tailoring in the servicing sector showed more than 30 per cent of the households crossing the poverty line. In the laundry enterprise, out of seven entrepreneurs assisted, no one crossed the poverty line.

(v) Shift of Beneficiaries to Higher Income Groups

The income of the members has been categorised into four groups. It is not possible to expect all the four groups of poor people to cross the poverty line. One can consider that some progress is achieved if a household moves from a lower income group to a higher income group. An overall upward shift of income of the members is shown in Table—6.22 and Figure 6.4.

Table—6.22 Upward income shift of members

(No. of members)

		Post credit year					
	Income range in rupees	*Below Rs. 5000*	*Rs. 5000 – Rs. 10000*	*Rs. 10000 – Rs. 11500*	*Rs. 11500 – Rs. 13600*	*Rs. 13600 and above*	*Number of members*
	1	2	3	4	5	6	7
Base Year	Below Rs. 5000	2 (2.4)	58 (70.7)	6 (7.3)	8 (9.8)	8 (9.8)	82 (32.3)
	Rs. 5000-Rs. 10000	–	45 (36.0)	22 (17.6)	31 (24.8)	27 (21.6)	125 (49.2)
	Rs. 10000-Rs. 11500	–	–	–	2 (33.3)	4 (66.7)	6 (2.4)
	Rs. 11500-13600	–	–	–	2 (16.7)	10 (83.3)	12 (4.7)
	Rs. 13600 and above	–	–	–	–	29 (100.00)	29 (11.4)
	Total	**2 (0.8)**	**103 (40.6)**	**28 (11.0)**	**43 (16.9)**	**78 (30.7)**	**254 (100.00)**

Figures in brackets denote percentage to total.

For the purpose of this assessment, net income of the member is used. The income slabs are less than Rs. 5,000, Rs. 5,001-10,000, Rs. 10,001-11,500, Rs. 11,501-13,600, Rs. 13,600 and above. The data in Table—6.22 depicts the frequency distribution of members in different income ranges. The two points of time used are base year and post credit year.

It is evident from Table—6.22 that the first two of the lower income groups (less than Rs. 10,000) have experienced a decline in number of members in the post-credit compared to the base year. The percentage decline of the income group of less than Rs. 5,000 was 97.56 over the base year. Similarly, in the next higher income groups the decline was 17.6 per cent. In the remaining income group i.e Rs. 10,001, Rs. 11,501, Rs. 13,600 and Rs. 13,600 and above there has been a corresponding increase in the post credit year over the base year. In terms of percentages, the increase is 300,258 and 168.97 respectively.

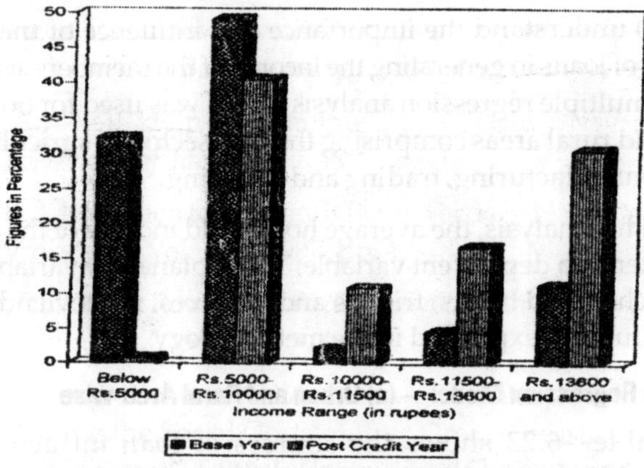

Fig. 6.4: Upward Income Shift of Members

It could also be observed from Table—6.22 that out of 82 members who were in the income group below Rs. 5,000 in the base year, 58 members (70.7 per cent) had been shifted to the next income group, six members (7.3 per cent) to Rs. 10,000 - Rs. 11,500 income group, eight members (9.8 per cent) to Rs. 11,501 - Rs. 13,600 income group and the remaining members to Rs. 13,601 and above income group. Out of 125 members who were in the Rs. 5,001 - Rs. 10,000 income group, 45 members (36 per cent) remained in the same group, 22 members (17.6 per cent) have shifted to the third group of income, 31 members (24.8 per cent) to the fourth income group and 27 persons (21.6 per cent) to the fifth group which is the highest range of income. Out of six members who were in the income group in the base year Rs. 10,001-Rs. 11,500, two members (33.3 per cent) have shifted to next income group and four members (66.7 per cent) to the income group of Rs. 13,601 and above. Thus the above analysis shows that the shifting of the members in the income ladder from the lower to the higher income group is impressive and substantial.

(vi) Sources of Credits and the Determinants Influencing the Household Income of the Members—Regression Analysis

In this section an attempt has been made to assess the impact of micro-credit on the income levels of the micro entrepreneurs in the Self Help Groups. Two multiple regression models were carried out (i) to find out the impact of major sources of credit on the average household income of the members, (ii) to find out the major determinants of average household income of the micro entrepreneurs.

To understand the importance and influence of the various sources of loans in generating the income of the members at different levels, multiple regression analysis model was used for both urban slum and rural areas comprising the four sectors—agriculture and allied, manufacturing, trading and servicing.

In his analysis, the average household income of the member was taken as a dependent variable. The explanatory variables were SHG, scheduled banks, friends and relatives, moneylenders, and corpus fund as explained in the methodology.

Multiple Regression Model— (a) Urban and Rural Area-wise

Table—6.23 shows the sources of loan influencing the household income of the members by using regression analysis in the urban and rural areas.

Table—6.23 Estimated co-efficient of the major sources of credit influencing the income of the members—multiple regression analysis

	Urban (N–121)		*Rural (N–133)*	
Variables	*Co-efficient*	*'t' value*	*Co-efficient*	*'t' value*
SHGs	2.3289	3.657**	3.2008	4.690**
Scheduled Banks	0.1735	8.934**	0.3416	0.904
Corpus fund	1.0509	1.229	2.2131	1.574
Friends and Relatives	-0.5622	1.022	0.6428	0.856
Moneylenders	–	–	-0.1077	0.492
R^2	0.43754		0.3589	
't' value	22.5590**		4.7988**	
Intercept	8306.8038		7632.2574	

It could be observed that an increase in the loan from SHGs by one rupee leads to an increase in average income of the number by Rs. 2.33 in the case of urban slums and Rs. 3.20 in the case of rural areas. An increase in the loan from scheduled banks by one rupee leads to an increase in average income of the number by Rs. 0.17 in the urban area and Rs. 0.34 in the rural areas. Both the variables were statistically significant in the urban areas. The variable SHGs was found to be significant at one per cent level and the variable scheduled banks was found to be not significant in the rural areas. Though the increase in the loan from the corpus fund leads to increase in income of the number, it was not statistically significant in either of the areas. The increase in loan from friends and relatives led to decrease in average income of the member in the urban area and to an increase in average income of the member in the rural area and this was not statistically significant. The co-efficient of variation in case of moneylenders was found to be negative in the rural area. The estimated multiple correlation in case of urban slums R^2 is 0.43754 showing that 43.75 per cent of variations are explained by the above independent variables and the 't' value was 22.5590, which was statistically significant at one per cent level, whereas in the case of rural area, R^2 was 0.3589 showing that 35.89 per cent and the 't' value was 4.7988, which was statistically significant at one per cent level. So, the above analysis reveals that the above said variables influenced the average income of the member.

Multiple Regression Model—(b) Agriculture and Allied Sector

Table—6.24 Estimated co-efficients of the major sources of credit (Agriculture and Allied Sector)

Variables	*Co-efficient*	*'t' value*
SHGs	3.3540	2.606*
Scheduled banks	3.0138	1.399
Corpus fund	-3.3998	0.798
Friends and relatives	4.9411	2.040*
Intercept	2289.9417	
R^2—0.5013		
't' value–4.6898**		

No. of members—23.

* Significant at five per cent level.

It could be noted that the multiple regression co-efficient R^2 is 0.5103, signifying that 51.03 per cent of variations in average income of the member are explained by the selected independent variables included in the model. The co-efficient of the variables SHGs and friends and relatives were significant at five per cent level, whereas the variables such as scheduled banks and corpus fund were not significant.

An expected finding is that a one rupee increase in loan from the SHGs leads to an increase in the average income of the member by Rs. 3.35. A one rupee increase in the loan from the source friends and relatives leads to increase in average income of the member by Rs. 4.94. Another expected finding is that an increase in the bank loan positively influences the income of the member by Rs. 3.01. Though it is not statistically significant, it indirectly reinforces the findings that the women in the agricultural sector mostly depend on SHGs and friends and relatives and the members avail loan from banks when they are in need. An increase in the corpus fund leads to a decrease in the average income of the member by Rs. 3.40 because the number of members receiving the assistance from corpus fund under agricultural sector is very less. The 't' value is calculated and it is significant at one per cent level (4.6898). This indicates that R^2 is significant. Therefore, it may be concluded that the selected independent variables were significantly influencing the changes in average income of the members.

Multiple Regression Model—(c) Manufacturing Sector

In this sector, the average net income of the member is a dependent variable whereas SHGs, scheduled banks, corpus fund, friends and relatives were explanatory variables. With the multiple regression function, it is possible to measure the effect of the constant.

Table—6.25 clearly shows that one rupee increase in the bank loan leads to an increase in the average net income of the member by Rs. 0.16 and it is statistically significant at one per cent level. Another expected finding is that an increase in the SHG leads to an increase in the average net income of the member by Rs. 1.99 and this variable is significant at one per cent level. The increase in loan from the sources friends and relatives and corpus funds scheme leads to decrease in the average net income of the member by Rs. 0.022 and Rs. 1.07, and these two variables are not significantly significant. The co-efficient of multiple correlation R^2 is 0.5071, explaining 50.71 per cent of variation in the average net income of the member. The 'f' value was 18.52 which is significant at one per cent level. Therefore, to increase the income of the members it is necessary to increase the amount of loan through various sources by formulating appropriate micro credit and supporting policies for development.

Table—6.25 Multiple regression analysis (Manufacturing sector)

Variables	*Co-efficient*	*'t' value*
SHGs	1.9898	2.484**
Scheduled banks	0.1609	8.126**
Corpus fund	-1.0701	0.919
Friends and relatives	-0.2213	0.334
Intercept	10230.2906	
R^2 value	0.5071	
't' value	18.52**	

No. of members—77.

Multiple Regression Model—(d) Trading Sector

The dependent variable in this sector is the average net household income of the member. The independent variables are SHGs, scheduled banks, corpus fund, friends and relatives and moneylenders. To study the impact of micro credit on average household income of the member under trading is shown in Table—6.26.

Table—6.26 Multiple regression analysis (Trading sector)

Variables	*Co-efficient*	*'t' value*
SHGs	1.8315	2.717**
Scheduled banks	0.4562	3.706**
Corpus fund	1.8519	1.787
Friends and relatives	-0.0083	-0.011
Money lenders	-0.1121	-0.517
Intercept	8947.1347	
R^2	0.4611	
'f' value	4.7615**	

No. of members—130.

It is observed that the estimated co-efficient of the variables bank loan, SHGs are significant at one per cent level. The co-efficient of the variables corpus fund, moneylenders, friends and relatives are not significant. If an increase in bank loan per member leads to an increase in average net income of the members by Re. 0.46, the increase in SHG lending by one rupee per member leads to an increase in average net income of the member by Rs. 1.83. Though the co-efficient of variable corpus fund is not significant, one rupee increase in corpus fund leads to an increase in average income of the member by Rs. 1.85. An expected finding is that an increase in loan from moneylenders leads to decrease in income of the member due to high rate of interest, ranging between 36 to 60 per cent per annum. An increase in the variable, friends and relatives leads to decrease in the average net income of the number. The co-efficient multiple correlation R^2 is 0.4611 showing that 46.11 per cent of variations are explained by the above independent variables. The 'f' value is 4.7615. This indicates that the income of the members was influenced by their borrowing from the above mentioned sources.

Multiple Regression Model—(e) Servicing Sector

In this sector, the average net income of the member in the servicing sector is taken as a dependent variable. The independent variables are SHGs, scheduled banks, corpus fund, friends and relatives and moneylenders. With the multiple regression, it is possible to measure the net effect of the constant.

Table—6.27 Multiple regression analysis (Servicing sector)

Variables	*Co-efficient*	*'t' value*
SHGs	6.1921	4.387**
Scheduled banks	0.2745	0.212
Corpus fund	4.7591	1.808
Friends and relatives	-0.6061	0.449
Moneylenders	2.5261	1.914
Intercept	1081.6138	
R^2	0.55927	
'f' value	4.5683**	

No. of members—24.

It could be observed that an increase in the SHG lending per member leads to an increase in the average income of the member by Rs. 6.19 and it is statistically significant at one per cent level. The estimate of bank loan, moneylender's loan and corpus fund shows a positive contribution to the average net income of the member. One rupee increase in bank loan, moneylenders loan and corpus fund of the member results in an increase in the average net income of the member by Rs. 0.27, Rs. 2.53 and Rs. 4.76 respectively. However, these variables are not significant as the number of members benefited through these sources would be less. The estimate of average loan from friends and relatives shows a negative contribution to the income of the member and it is not statistically significant. Moreover, the co-efficient multiple correlation R^2 is 0.55927 showing that 52.92 per cent of variations are explained by the above independent variables. The 't' value was 4.5683 and it is statistically significant. This indicates that the average net income of the members was influenced by the said variables.

Multiple Regression Model—(f) Overall

An overall attempt has been made to assess the impact of micro credit on the income level of members. For this purpose average household income of the member was used as the independent variable. The independent variables were SHGs, scheduled banks, corpus fund, friends and relatives and moneylenders. The multiple regression analysis of micro credit for all the micro enterprises is shown in Table—6.28.

Table—6.28 Multiple regression analysis (Overall)

Variables	*Co-efficient*	*'t' value*
SHGs	2.5898	5.621**
Scheduled banks	0.1725	8.449**
Corpus fund	0.9810	1.366
Friends and relatives	-0.0523	0.117
Moneylenders	-0.0287	0.140
Intercept	8485.1266	
R^2	0.4882	
'f' value	20.0792**	

No. of members—254.

It could be noted that the estimated co-efficient of the variables SHGs scheduled banks are significant at one per cent level while the variables corpus fund, friends and relatives and moneylenders are not significant. It could also be observed that the increase in the loan from the sources of SHGs, scheduled banks and corps fund leads to an increase in the average income of the member while the loan from friends and relatives and moneylenders leads to decrease in the average income of the member as these source involved a high rate of interest and shorter repayment period. Moreover, whatever the amount repaid by the borrowers, it was treated as interest adjustment and not as the repayment of the principal amount. The co-efficient multiple correlation R^2 is 0.4882 showing that 48.82 per cent of variations are explained by the above independent variables. The 't' value was 20.0792 and it was statistically significant at one per cent level. This indicates that the average household income of the members was influenced by the various sources of loan.

Multiple Regression Model II

An overall analysis of all the micro enterprises among different sectors, as well as among rural and urban areas has been done. In the regression model II (Table—6.29) the average income of the member was considered as a dependent variable. The explanatory variables were (i) average loan, (ii) average own fund, (iii) average assets, (iv) average mandays, (v) average interest paid, (vi) average household expenses, and (vii) average education level of entrepreneurs.

Table—6.29 Multiple regression analysis—dependent variable average income of the entrepreneur (Model II)

	Variables	*Regression Co-efficient*	*'t' value*
1	*2*	3	4
1.	Average loan	0.3057	2.230**
2.	Average own funds	0.2005	3.091**
3.	Average assets	0.1550	2.290*
4.	Average employment (mandays)	1.8679	1.392

(Table Contd...)

1	2	3	4
5.	Average interest paid	-2.7802	1.818
6.	Average household expenses	81.2886	0.485
7.	Average education of entrepreneurs	27.1095	0.153
	Intercept	3100.6035	
	R^2	0.5445	
	'f' value	2.02361*	

No. of members–254.

* Significant at 5 per cent level.

In the regression model II estimated results are on the expected line. It is expected that an increase in loan per member leads to an increase in the average household income. The co-efficient estimate showed that one rupee increase in the loan per member leads to an increase in income by Rs. 0.31. An increase in the own funds per member leads to an increase in the average household income. Another expected finding is that, an increase in value of asset per member and that in mandays per member positively should influence average income of the household. On an average, one year of additional education leads to an increase of income around Rs. 27.11. An increase in the interest paid per member leads to a decrease in income of the household by Rs. 2.78. An increase in household expenses of the member contributes positively to the increase in income per member. Of these variables discussed, the variables average loan, average own funds are significant at one per cent level and the variable average incremental asset is significant at five per cent level. The other variables included are not statistically significant. The co-efficient of multiple regression R^2 is 0.5445. It showed that 54.5 per cent of variation is explained by the above independent variables. The 'f' value was 2.02361 and it is significant at five per cent level. This indicates that R^2 is significant. Therefore, it may be concluded that the selected independent variables were relevant for explaining the variations in income of the member.

(d) Asset Generation

Impact on Asset Position

Micro enterprises for the Self Help Group women aims at improving the lot of the poor women by creative new productive assets for them by giving necessary financial assistance. The hard core of poverty exists among the women of socially and economically backward classes. To emancipate such women from poverty, productive assets, which generate employment and income must be given to them. Therefore, under micro-credit scheme, Self Help Group women are enabled to acquire productive assets with the help of the loan from different sources such as SHGs, scheduled banks, corpus fund, friends and relatives and moneylenders. The financial assistance availed by the entrepreneurs shall not be diverted but be used to serve the designated asset and the asset shall be maintained and operated so as to derive income. Only then can be beneficiaries move above the poverty line. Assets would include land and containers for detergent making, machinery and tools for cottage industry, animals for dairy, vessels for food processing and catering, sewing machines for tailoring, sheep and goat for rearing, racks for petty shop, cupboard and almirah for sale of cloth, carts for vegetable and fruits vending, grinders for grinding, etc. The entrepreneurs may improve their assets-base if they are able to reinvest a part of the incremental income. Hence an attempt is made in this section to study the economic reforms from micro enterprises undertaken by the Self Help Group members in creating an additional asset-base to entrepreneurs household.

Area-wise Asset Position

The area-wise asset position of the micro entrepreneurs is shown in Table—6.30.

It is clear from Table—6.30 that the magnitude of additional assets is almost same among the two areas. Though the percentage of increase in assets seems to be relatively high for urban areas (333.83 per cent) when compared with rural area groups (293.16 per cent), in absolute terms, the increase in the value of assets of micro entrepreneurs belonging to urban area groups was Rs. 4,352.73 with standard deviation of Rs. 16,945.86, while the micro entrepreneurs of rural area groups occupy the next position with an increase of Rs. 4,044.74 with the standard deviation of 7456.48. The 't' values revealed that there was a positive impact of investment on asset position as the 't' values were statistically significant.

Table—6.30 **Area-wise average value of assets possessed by the entrepreneurs in the base year and post credit year**

(Value in Rupees)

S. No.	Area	Base year		Post credit year		Incremental assets		Percentage variation	Paired 't' value
		Mean	Standard deviation	Mean	Standard deviation	Mean	Standard deviation		
1.	Urban	1303.88	2461.25	5656.61	19315.51	4352.73	16945.86	333.83	2.83**
2.	Rural	1379.70	1942.13	5424.44	8470.00	4044.74	7456.48	293.16	6.26***
	Total	**1343.58**	**2200.59**	**5535.04**	**14642.49**	**4191.46**	**12854.39**	**311.96**	**5.20****

Asset Position—Micro Enterprise-wise

The data relating to assets generated in various micro enterprises of the study area are presented in Table—6.31. The average value of all the assets possessed by the entrepreneurs in the base year and post credit year are shown in the table. As a matter of fact, the increase in the value of the assets in each enterprise shall not be less than the total investment made, on the average, by a family. The financial assistance and own funds invested in the grounding of the project are used as fixed capital and working capital. Under such circumstances, the increase in the value of productive assets will be less than the total funds utilised in the enterprises. The increase in the value of assets will also be less than the financial assistance secured, as a part or as the whole funds are diverted for other purposes. Sometimes, the incremental assets will be more than the investment, this reveals that the entrepreneurs have reinvested a part of their income in procuring new asset or additional assets.

It is evident, from Table—6.31 that the average value of assets has been increased during the post credit period in the case of all the micro enterprises. Taking all the scheme together, the average asset-holding of entrepreneurs has increased from Rs. 1343.58 to Rs. 5535.04 indicating 311.96 per cent increase in post credit year. Micro enterprise-wise analysis revealed that the asset creation was high in the case of detergent-making followed by tailoring and dairy farming. The three enterprises in the agricultural sector and the increase in the value of assets in the post credit year is highly satisfactory. In the manufacturing sector, the highest increase (511.78 per cent) was in detergent-making. In the trading sector, the percentage increase in the value of the assets was about 300 per cent in the case of petty shop and sale of cloth. In the agricultural and allied sector, dairy farming showed highest incremental assets (310.20 per cent). In trading sector the highest incremental asset was shown in the case of sale of cloth (341.72 per cent) and in the servicing sector, the tailoring unit revealed the highest incremental asset. This shows that whatever income was earned in this unit was reinvested in procuring additional assets. Statistically the average additional value of assets was found to be significant in the case of all the micro enterprises, except detergent-making and

Table—6.31 Enterprise-wise average value of assets possessed by the micro entrepreneurs in the base year and post credit year

(in rupees)

S. No.	Sector/Micro Enterprises	Base year		Post credit year		Incremental assets		Percentage variation	Paired 't' values
		Mean	SD	Mean	SD	Mean	SD		
I.	**Agriculture and allied**	2204.35	249.39	7530.43	7326.88	5326.09	6162.97	241.62	4.14**
	1. Dairy farming	2450.00	2565.26	10050.00	9346.57	7600.00	7834.39	310.20	3.07**
	2. Poultry	1250.00	812.84	4250.00	4559.14	3000.00	4159.76	240.00	2.04
	3. Sheep and goat rearing	3240.00	3855.26	7740.00	4987.79	4500.00	3989.99	138.00	2.52**
II.	**Manufacturing**	1441.17	3265.62	6862.99	23656.70	5421.82	20612.73	376.21	2.31*
	1. Cottage industries	1065.22	879.88	5434.78	7546.02	4369.57	7135.47	410.20	2.94**
	2. Detergent making	1966.00	5454.54	12027.50	44278.06	10061.50	38852.55	511.78	1.16
	3. Food processing/catering	1386.76	2577.92	4791.18	10004.83	3404.41	7579.55	245.49	2.62**
III.	**Trading**	1007.69	891.25	4045.77	5991.86	3038.08	5738.42	301.49	6.04**
	1. Petty shop	1158.11	898.73	4878.38	6390.93	3720.27	6014.98	321.24	3.76**
	2. Sale of cloth	1010.87	843.93	4465.22	7906.29	3454.35	7731.81	341.72	3.03**
	3. Sale of food items	886.17	930.27	2979.79	2381.78	2093.62	2022.53	236.25	7.10**
IV.	**Servicing**	2025.00	2396.42	7429.17	15175.82	5404.17	13311.37	266.87	1.99
	1. Tailoring	2290.91	2858.48	11736.36	21994.42	9445.45	19217.51	412.30	1.63
	2. Grinding	1666.67	1751.19	3583.33	2973.49	1916.67	1828.02	114.99	2.57*
	3. Laundry	1914.29	2359.68	3957.14	2519.16	2042.85	2376.17	106.72	2.27*
	Total	**1343.58**	**2200.59**	**5535.04**	**14642.49**	**4191.46**	**12854.39**	**311.96**	**5.20****

Note: *Significant at five per cent level.

tailoring as the computed 't' values were significant at one per cent level and five per cent level respectively. Thus the results reveal that all the micro enterprises have made an excellent impact in terms of additional asset creation.

Relationship Between Investment and Asset Position

The relationship between investment and asset position of the micro entrepreneurs is studied by using correlation analysis.

Table—6.32 Investment and asset position relationship—area-wise (Correlation Analysis)

Area	*Correlation Co-efficient*
Urban	0.9283**
Rural	0.6670**

The correlation analysis (Table—6.32) shows that correlation is highly significant at one per cent level both in the case of urban and rural areas. There is a positive relationship between investment and asset position of the micro entrepreneurs in both the areas.

Table—6.33 Investment and asset position relationship—sector-wise (Correlation Analysis)

Sector	*Correlation Co-efficient*
Agriculture and allied	0.3964
Manufacturing	0.9564**
Trading	0.4985**
Servicing	0.6739**

From Table—6.33 it was observed that correlation is significant at one per cent level in all the sectors except agriculture and allied sector. But the relationship between investment and asset position is positively correlated in all the sectors. The relationship is highly correlated in case of manufacturing sector (0.9564).

Table—6.34 Investment and asset position relationship—micro enterprises-wise (Correlation Analysis)

Micro enterprises	*Co-efficient correlation*
Dairy farming	0.3261
Poultry farming	0.2090
Sheep rearing	0.7737
Cottage industries	0.2140
Detergent making	0.9993**
Food processing/catering	0.7536**
Petty shop	0.3492**
Sale of cloth	0.5475**
Sale of food items	0.7435**
Tailoring	0.8854**
Grinding	0.3358
Laundry	0.5609

* Significant at five per cent level.

The correlation analysis (Table—6.34) explains that the co-efficient correlation is significant at one per cent level in the case of detergent making, food processing/catering, sale of cloth, sale of food items and tailoring, and it is significant at five per cent level in the case of petty shop. The relationship between investment and asset position is positively correlated in all the enterprises. The correlation is highly (0.9993) in the case of detergent making and has a low correlation in the case of poultry farming.

Impact of Investment on Asset Generated

To study the impact of investment on asset position of the micro enterprises under different sectors, regression analysis was fitted. Table—6.35 shows the impact of investment on the additional asset position sector-wise.

Table—6.35 Impact of investment on asset position—sector-wise

S. No.	*Sector*	*Co-efficient*	R^2	*'t' value*
1.	Agriculture and allied	0.3494	0.1803	0.84
2.	Manufacturing	0.5424	0.9617	30.42**
3.	Trading	0.4995	0.4883	6.33**
4.	Servicing	2.6142	0.6593	4.113**

It is evident from Table—6.35 that the elasticity co-efficient of investment, when placed in relation to increase in assets was 0.3494 for agricultural sector, 0.5424 for manufacturing sector, 0.4995 for trading sector and 2.6142 for servicing sector. This indicates that all the co-efficients, except in the agricultural sector, were significantly different from zero at the probability level of one per cent. To sum up, the elasticity co-efficient of the investments on assets are positive.

Table—6.36 Impact of investment on asset position—area-wise

S. No.	*Sector*	*Co-efficient*	R^2	*'t' value*
1.	Urban	0.5329	0.9277	27.11**
2.	Rural	1.2291	0.6516	9.83**
	Overall	0.5444	0.8720	28.275**

The area-wise results of the impact of investment on additional assets position is presented in Table—6.36. It can be observed from the table that the elasticity co-efficient on investment, when placed in relation to increase in assets, were 0.5329 for urban area entrepreneurships and 1.2291 for rural entrepreneurs. It also states that all the co-efficients were significant at one per cent level. It means the elasticity co-efficients of investment on assets were positive. An expected findings is that an increase in investment per member leads to an increase in the incremental assets. Thus the co-efficient estimate showed that one rupee increase in the investment per member leads to an increase in assets by Re. 0.54. This is a significant finding from the point of view of micro credit institutions and from the point of women members.

(d) Employment Generation

Income generation is the major thrust of the micro credit programme for the Self Help Group women. This programme is initiated to promote micro-enterprises for the benefit of the rural and urban poor women. The micro-entrepreneurs are provided with financial assistance to acquire a productive asset and the creation, maintenance and operation of such an asset is expected to generate employment of the beneficiaries. As far as employment generation is concerned, the benefit is to be estimated in terms of additional mandays of employment created for the beneficiaries. There are also difficulties in estimating employment generation in micro enterprises, as the micro entrepreneurs work in the project according to their convenience. Subject to these limitations, the impact of micro enterprises on employment generation is analysed.

Area-wise Employment Generation

To assess the differential impact of any of the micro entrepreneurs belonging to both urban slum and rural groups the data were disaggregated area-wise, as shown in Table—6.37.

Table—6.37 Area-wise average entrepreneurial employment (Mandays) in the base and post credit year

(in mandays)

S. No.	Area	Base year		Post credit year		Incremental assets		Percentage variation	Paired 't' value
		Mean	Standard deviation	Mean	Standard deviation	Mean	Standard deviation		
1.	Urban	149.88	36.12	199.62	75.43	49.74	65.68	33.19	8.33**
2.	Rural	170.29	58.29	212.05	93.60	41.76	76.23	24.52	6.32**
	Total	**160.57**	**49.96**	**206.12**	**85.49**	**45.56**	**71.37**	**28.37**	**10.17****

It can be observed from Table—6.37 that the percentage increase in average employment was highest for micro entrepreneurs belonging to urban slum groups (33.19 per cent) followed by rural self help group members (24.52 per cent). The additional mean employment created in terms of mandays was 199.62, with standard deviation 75.43 for urban slum micro entrepreneurs and in the case of rural entrepreneurs, it was 212.05 with a standard deviation of 93.60. The incremental employment was to be significant at one per cent level in case of both urban and rural areas as indicated by the 't' values in the above table.

Enterprise-wise Employment Generation

The data relating to the average employment of the micro entrepreneurs among various enterprises during the base and post credit year are presented in Table—6.38.

Table—6.38 Sector-wise average employment (Mandays) in the base year and post credit year among entrepreneurs

(Mandays)

S. No.	Sector/Micro Enterprises	Base year		Post credit year		Incremental assets		Percentage variation	Paired 't' values
		Mean	SD	Mean	SD	Mean	SD		
I.	**Agriculture**	169.09	55.70	198.68	59.16	29.59	46.32	17.50	3.06**
	1. Dairy farming	160.30	66.88	183.90	72.77	15.60	51.60	9.73	0.96
	2. Poultry	167.88	56.36	214.17	55.56	46.29	47.51	27.57	2.76*
	3. Sheep and goat rearing	172.60	37.72	203.47	29.60	30.87	28.49	17.89	2.42
II.	**Manufacturing**	155.92	42.62	211.85	85.96	55.93	75.31	35.87	6.52**
	1. Cottage industries	158.61	39.97	225.87	89.84	67.26	77.27	42.41	4.17**
	2. Detergent making	162.00	68.65	245.27	91.45	83.27	85.20	41.40	4.37**
	3. Food processing/catering	150.53	19.65	182.72	71.64	32.19	61.48	21.38	3.05**
III.	**Trading**	164.94	56.12	207.36	92.70	42.42	74.71	25.72	6.47**
	1. Petty shop	160.62	51.70	215.83	79.70	55.21	60.20	34.37	5.58**
	2. Sale of cloth	160.62	53.49	187.51	91.59	26.89	82.60	16.74	2.21**
	3. Sale of food items	172.57	62.02	220.11	101.51	47.54	75.79	27.55	4.30**
IV.	**Servicing**	143.58	14.62	188.19	62.71	44.61	57.08	31.07	3.83**
	1. Tailoring	145.55	16.89	207.70	74.62	62.15	67.86	42.70	3.04**
	2. Grinding	138.50	17.33	145.67	16.79	7.17	16.13	5.17	1.09
	3. Laundry	144.86	7.69	194.00	54.88	49.14	51.00	33.92	2.55*
	Total	**160.57**	**49.96**	**206.12**	**85.49**	**45.56**	**71.37**	**28.37**	**10.17****

Note: *Significant at five per cent level.

The average employment had increased during the post credit year for beneficiaries at all the micro enterprises. Taking all the sectors together, the average employment have increased from 160.57 to 206.12 mandays indicating 28.37 per cent increase with the standard deviation 71.37. Among the various micro enterprises, detergent powder making recorded the highest increase (51.40 per cent) with standard deviation followed by tailoring (42.70 per cent) and cottage industries (42.41 per cent). From the data it appeared that detergent powder making and tailoring enterprises had provided more mandays of employment, both in the base year and post credit year compared to all the other enterprises. The incremental mandays of employment had exceeded 75 in the cottage industries and detergent making. These two enterprises were more labour-intensive than the both enterprises. In the trading sector, petty shop business created more mandays (55.21 mandays) than other enterprises in the sector. Next came the sale of food items, which created additional employment of 47.54 mandays. From Table—6.38 the statistical results indicate that the additional mandays of employment were found to be significant in the case of all the micro enterprises except dairy farming, and sheep rearing as the number of entrepreneurs under this scheme was very less.

Relationship Between Investment and Employment Generation (Mandays)

The relationship between investment and employment generation in terms of mandays of the micro entrepreneurs is analysed by using correlation analysis.

Table—6.39 Investment-employment generation (mandays)—area-wise (correlation analysis)

Area	*Correlation Co-efficient*
Urban	0.1065
Rural	0.2479

The correlation analysis (Table—6.39) explains that the correlation is not significant in both the areas, but the relationship between investment and employment generation is positively correlated.

Table—6.40 Investment-employment generation (mandays)—sector-wise (correlation analysis)

Sector	*Correlation Co-efficient*
Agriculture and allied	0.3007*
Manufacturing	0.2538**
Trading	0.1032
Servicing	0.1764

Note: *Significant at five per cent level.

From the Table—6.40 it could be observed that the correlation is significant at one per cent level in the case of manufacturing sector and is significant at five per cent level in the case of agricultural and allied sectors, whereas the correlation is not significant in trading and servicing sectors. But the relationship between investment and employment generation is positively correlated in all the sectors.

Table—6.41 Investment-employment generation relationship—micro enterprises-wise (correlation analysis)

Micro Enterprises	*Co-efficient Correlation*
Dairy farming	0.6055**
Poultry farming	0.0286
Sheep rearing	0.1930
Cottage industries	0.2102
Detergent making	0.3995**
Food processing/catering	0.3188
Petty shop	0.1144
Sale of cloth	0.1945
Sale of food items	0.0533
Tailoring	-0.4174
Grinding	-0.1750
Laundry	0.2523

The correlation analysis in Table—6.41 shows that the co-efficient correlation is significant at one per cent level in the case of dairy farming and detergent making, whereas the correlation is not significant in all the other enterprises. The relationship between investment and employment generation is positively correlated in all the enterprises, except tailoring and grinding. The correlation is low in the case of poultry farming and sale of food items.

(f) Recovery Performance

More than 50 per cent of the micro entrepreneurs still buy their raw materials on a daily basis. Nearly a quarter of them are involved in weekly purchases. This high turnover of raw material transactions manifests the importance of working capital. When the working capital in an enterprise is of utmost importance, the sources of credit should be highly borrower-friendly. They should be easily accessible, offer flexible terms of repayment, low rate of interest, be free from formalities and collateral. The field data reveals that 75 per cent of the borrowings are utilised to meet the working capital needs. While the enterprises are involved in daily and weekly purchases of raw materials and sales realisation, the loan repayment is in the mode of monthly schedule. Actually, the respondents have funds enough to honour weekly repayment of the loan dues. But, as a matter of convenience and saving of time, they prefer a monthly repayment schedule.

The micro entrepreneurs had depended on various sources for credit to finance the micro enterprises. The credit was contributed from the SHGs bank loan, private loan, own sources. A part of the incremental income arising out of the operation of the enterprises had to be utilised to repay the loan given by the financial institutions as per the repayment schedule fixed by the authorities. Since the loan had to be repaid, the financial assistance had to be productively used by the beneficiaries. Prompt repayment of funds would enable the financial institutions to recycle their funds. An important criteria for the success of the micro enterprises is the recovery of the loan advanced to the entrepreneurs. It may be understood that the repayment schedule varies between 12 to 36 months. In the case of bank loan the repayment has to commerce after the lapse of a certain period known as gestation period but in the case of the credit lent by SHGs, the repayment commences the very next month. The repayment pattern has been analysed after the expiry of two years and in some of the enterprises the repayment period is not yet over.

The tables given in this section indicate the comparative repayment performance of micro entrepreneurs.

The pattern of repayment of loans area-wise is shown in Table—6.42.

Table—6.42 Area-wise pattern of repayment of loan

S. No.	Area	Number of entrepreneurs	Number of entrepreneurs repaid in full	Number of entrepreneurs repaid partially		Number entrepreneurs who did not repay at all
				Below 50%	Above 50%	
1.	Urban	121 (100.00)	9 (7.44)	23 (19.00)	88 (72.73)	1 (0.83)
2.	Rural	133 (100.00)	2 (1.50)	32 (24.06)	99 (74.44)	–
	Total	**254 (100.00)**	**11 (4.33)**	**55 (21.65)**	**187 (73.62)**	**1 (0.39)**

It could be seen from Table—6.42 that 4.33 per cent of the entrepreneurs have repaid the loan in full, 73.62 per cent repaid more than 50 per cent and 21.65 per cent of the entrepreneurs repaid less than 50 per cent of the loan. Among the urban slum entrepreneurs, 19 per cent repaid below 50 per cent, 72.73 per cent repaid more than 50 per cent, 7.44 per cent repaid the loan in full. About 74.44 per cent of the entrepreneurs belonging to rural area repaid above 50 per cent of the loan and 24.06 per cent repaid less than 50 per cent. It was encouraging to note that out of 254 entrepreneurs only one had not started repayment at all.

Enterprise-wise Repayment Performance

The pattern of repayment of loan enterprise-wise is shown in Table—6.43.

When all the sectors are taken together, it is seen from Table—6.43 that 4.33 per cent of the entrepreneurs have repaid the loan in full and another 73.62 per cent have repaid more than 50 per cent of the loan. The highest repayment performance is seen in poultry farming (12.50 per cent) in the agricultural sector, and in

Table—6.43 Enterprise-wise pattern of repayment of loan

S. No.	Sector/Micro enterprises	Number of entrepreneurs repaid in full	Number of entrepreneurs repaid partially		Number of entrepreneurs who did not rapay in full	Total number of entrepreneurs
			Below 50%	Above 50%		
1	2	3	4	5	6	7
I.	**Agriculture and Allied**	2 (8.70)	3 (13.04)	18 (78.26)	–	23 (100.00)
	1. Dairy farming	1 (10.00)	2 (20.00)	7 (70.00)	–	10 (100.00)
	2. Poultry	1 (12.50)	–	7 (87.50)	–	8 (100.00)
	3. Sheep and goat rearing	–	1 (20.00)	4 (80.00)	–	5 (100.00)
II.	**Manufacturing**	2 (2.60)	17 (22.08)	58 (75.32)	–	77 (100.00)
	1. Cottage industry	–	3 (13.04)	20 (86.96)	–	23 (100.00)
	2. Detergent making	2 (10.00)	5 (25.00)	13 (65.00)	–	20 (100.00)
	3. Food processing/catering	–	9 (26.47)	25 (73.53)	–	34 (100.00)

(Table Contd...)

1	2	3	4	5	6	7
III.	**Trading**	6 (4.62)	31 (23.85)	92 (70.77)	1 (0.77)	130 (100.00)
	1. Petty shop	2 (5.41)	8 (21.62)	26 (70.27)	1 (2.70)	37 (100.00)
	2. Sale of cloth	3 (6.52)	13 (23.26)	30 (65.62)	–	46 (100.00)
	3. Sale of food items	1 (2.13)	10 (21.28)	36 (76.60)	–	47 (100.00)
IV.	**Servicing**	1 (4.17)	4 (16.67)	19 (79.17)	–	24 (100.00)
	1. Tailoring	–	2 (18.18)	9 (81.82)	–	11 (100.00)
	2. Grinding	–	2 (33.33)	4 (66.67)	–	6 (100.00)
	3. Laundry	1 (14.29)	–	6 (85.71)	–	7 (100.00)
	Total	**11** **(4.33)**	**55** **(21.65)**	**187** **(73.62)**	**1** **(0.39)**	**254** **(100.00)**

Note: Figures in brackets denote percentage to total.

laundry in the servicing sector (14.29 per cent). All the entrepreneurs have paid more than 50 per cent of the loan.

In dairy farming the percentage of total repayers in full is 10. The entrepreneurs who repaid more than 50 per cent is 70; the entrepreneurs who repaid less than 50 per cent is 20. In poultry farming out of eight entrepreneurs 12.50 per cent of them have paid in full and 87.50 per cent have repaid more than 50 per cent. In sheep rearing, 80 per cent of the entrepreneurs have repaid more than 50 per cent of the loan.

In cottage industry 86.96 per cent of entrepreneurs have paid more than 50 per cent and 22.08 per cent have repaid less than 50 per cent of the loan. In the case of detergent-making 65 per cent have repaid more than 50 per cent and 25 per cent have repaid less than 50 per cent. In food processing/catering, 73.53 per cent of the entrepreneurs have paid more than 50 per cent of the loan and 26.47 per cent have paid less than 50 per cent.

In petty shop enterprises, out of 37 entrepreneurs two (5.41 per cent) have repaid in full, 26 (70.27 per cent) have repaid more than 50 per cent, eight (21.62 per cent) have repaid below 50 per cent and only one (2.70 per cent) has not rapaid at all. In sale of cloth and textile items, 65.62 per cent have repaid more than 50 per cent and 6.52 per cent have paid in full. In sale of food items 2.13 per cent of the entrepreneurs have paid the loan in full, 76.60 per cent have paid more than 50 per cent of the loan. In tailoring 81.82 per cent, in grinding 66.67 per cent and among the entrepreneurs in laundry 85.71 per cent have repaid more than 50 per cent of the loan.

The micro entrepreneurs belonging to agricultural sector as a whole, has fared better in repayment, i.e. 8.70 per cent have repaid in full and 78.26 per cent have repaid more than 50 per cent. In the trading and servicing sector, 4.62 per cent and 4.17 per cent have repaid in full and 70.77 per cent and 79.17 per cent of the entrepreneurs respectively, have repaid more than 50 per cent of the loan.

SECTION III

Social Benefits Accrued to the Members of SHGs

The micro-credit programme in the SHGs has brought about perceptible changes. As a result of participation in the micro-credit programme, a large number of women had taken up micro enterprises like manufacturing pickles, dairy, petty shops and diversification of agricultural activities. Consequently, family income had substantially increased. Apart from the economic changes, tremendous social changes in the project area targets were also observed. Women commanded more respect, got due affection and rightful place in the family. Positive empowerment of women was evident in their involvement in family decisions being markedly enhanced. As a group, women have gained more confidence and power. In many areas, they forced liquor shops to close. Strategic points are now patrolled by women who are in a position to chase away drunken men entering the village. Thus it has proved that micro lending for micro enterprises could be economically and socially viable.

The social benefits accrued to the members of the SHGs are discussed on the following lines:

A. Group dynamics of SHGs.

B. Degree of empowerment traits attained by the micro entrepreneurs.

C. Problems in implementing micro credit programme among SHGs.

(A) Group Dynamics of SHGs

The group's performance, to a large extent, is dependent on the promoting agency, i.e. the NGO, in the initial stages and in the long run on the resources that its members generate and accumulate for the group, size of the group, ability and performance of the group members, group cohesiveness, level of conflict and internal pressure on members to conform to the group's norms. The group has an internal structure that defines the rules and norms of members. The group structure and resources of the group members determine the interaction pattern and group behaviour.

Group dynamics is a field of study concerned with research and analysis of the various forces and patterns of formation of small informal groups. It includes such aspects as composition, interaction and behaviour of information groups. Kurt Edwin, a social psychologist of the IOWA University, USA laid the foundation of group dynamics as an academic and research discipline in 1930.

Group dynamics reflects the organisational behaviour exhibited by the groups. A score card with 20 criteria was prepared and administered to all the leaders of the SHGs. The outcomes of the SHGs in terms of group dynamics is discussed on the following sub headings:

I. Structure of the SHGs

II. Overall rating of SHGs

III. Benefits received from SHGs

(I) Structure of the SHGs

Table—6.44 gives details of the structure and performance of the SHGs

Table—6.44 Structure of the SHGs

S No.	*Aspects*	*Criteria*	*No. of groups*	
			Urban	*Rural*
1	2	3	4	5
1.	Group size	16-20 members 10-15 members	13 7	14 6
2.	Composition	Homogeneous Heterogeneous	20 –	20 –
3.	Caste representation	Mixed caste Single caste	15 5	2 18
4.	Leadership roles	Group leader + Secretary + Treasure Group leader + Treasure	20 –	20 –
5.	Group bye laws	Known to all members Known to most of the members Not known to the members	10 8 2	10 10 –

(Table Contd...)

1	2	3	4	5
6.	Attendance	More than 90 per cent	20	20
		Less than 90 per cent	–	–
7.	Participation in decision making	High	15	–
		Medium	5	9
		Low	–	11
8.	Savings pattern	Fixed amount	20	20
		Flexible amount	–	–
9.	Savings collection	Smooth	19	19
		Difficult	1	1
10.	On lending	Group has given first loan within second month	–	–
		First loan given between third and fifth month	20	20
		First loan given after six month	–	–
		Group has not started giving loan	–	–
11.	Rules for loaning	Group has eligibility criteria uniform for all members	20	–
		Eligibility criteria not uniform	–	20
12.	Interest rate	36% per annum	–	–
		24% per annum	–	1
		12% per annum	20	19
13.	Loan recovery index	100%	11	19
		95-99%	9	1
		Below 95%	–	–
14.	Documentation and reporting	Good	–	5
		Satisfactory	20	15
15.	Maintenance of records	Admission book	20	20
		Receipt book	20	20
		Pass book	20	20
		Savings and credit book	20	20
		Minutes book	20	20
16.	Awareness about schemes	Every member knows more than five schemes in which women can participate.	20	15
		Every member knownthree to four schemes in which women can participate	–	5

(Table Contd...)

1	2	3	4	5
17.	Access to other schemes	More than 10 members of the group have received benefits under other government schemes, training programmes, etc.	2	–
		Between 5-10 members of the group have received benefits under government schemes, training programme	18	20
18.	Role of NGO	The group is able to conduct its meetings without the help of NGO	–	–
		NGO helps in maintenance of records of the group	20	20
19.	Training programmes participated	Three	20	15
		Two	–	5
		None	–	–
20.	Awareness about bank details	Very good	–	–
		Satisfactory	20	20

The details given in Table—6.44 revealed the following:

- In the urban area, 13 groups and 14 groups from the rural areas had 16-20 members each. Only the remaining had less than 15 members.
- All the twenty groups in the urban as well as rural areas were found to be homogeneous.
- As many as 15 groups from the urban areas and five groups from the rural areas had mixed caste representation. The fact that 18 groups in the rural areas were constituted exclusively by a single caste, points to the rigid caste structure and affinity prevalent in the Indian villages.
- It was a happy augury that all the groups both in rural and urban areas functioned in the most democratic manner, with three representatives each.
- It is interesting to note that in 10 of the rural groups, the bye laws of SHGs were known to all the members. Surprisingly, in the urban areas, in eight out of the 20

groups the awareness of the bye laws was limited and two groups members did not know any of the bye laws mentioned in the group.

- It is a matter of great satisfaction that all the 20 groups in the urban as well as rural areas had more than 90 per cent attendance in their group meetings, indicating the regularity and good interaction, conducive to group dynamics.
- Among the 20 groups in the urban areas 13 reported a high degree of participation in decision-making. It was reported to be medium in the case of five SHGs in the urban areas and nine SHGs in the rural areas. The degree of participation was low in 11 of the rural groups, which may perhaps be due to the late formation of the SHGs themselves.
- All the urban and rural groups decided to save, ranging between Rs. 30 – Rs. 50 per month every month.
- With regard to the collection of savings, 19 groups in the urban areas and in the rural areas found in smooth sailing. In contrast only one group both in the urban area and in the rural area found it difficult to mobilise the collections regularly and voluntarily.
- All the 20 groups in both the areas commenced internal lending only after the third month.
- All the groups in the urban areas followed uniform rules for internal lending, which confirms groups cohesiveness. On the other hand, the rural SHGs did not have a uniform eligibility criteria.
- All the urban area SHGs and 19 out of the 20 groups in the rural area had agreed upon a nominal rate of interest (24 per cent p.a.) in order to mobilise more monetary returns to help other members.
- Recovery index works out to 100 per cent in the case of 11 urban groups and 19 rural groups, which was a positive trend indicating the integrity of the members.

- It is a matter of great satisfaction that all the groups had learnt the correct procedures for documentation and reporting to a satisfactory level owing to their exposure to the credit management training.
- In both the urban and rural areas all the groups maintained the registers and records expected of them, mainly due to the continuous monitoring of the groups by the researcher.
- The groups were given training or developmental inputs and schemes and, as a consequence, the members of all the groups in the urban areas and 15 groups in the rural areas were made aware of five to 10 developmental schemes, which is very encouraging as a mark of convergence. The remaining members became aware of three to four schemes.
- At least five to ten members of each of the groups in the rural sector and 18 of the groups in the urban sector claimed access to developmental schemes.
- Although the groups have been formed, they are still in the purpose of being stabilised, which requires a great deal of NGO intervention, particularly in the unkeep of records. This is revealed from the fact that all the groups conducted their day-to-day business independently but dependent on the NGO for scrutiny and guidance in updating their records.
- While all the urban SHGs had benefited from the training programme, only 15 SHGs from rural areas benefited from such experience.
- All the groups, both urban and rural, have became aware of bank procedures and formalities at least to a fairly satisfactory level, owing to the need to open and operate bank accounts.

(II) Overall Rating of the SHGs

When the overall scores were calculated the picture as depicted in Table—6.45 and Figure 6.5.

Table—6.45 Overall rating of the SHGs

Percentage scores	*Number of SHGs*	
	Urban N–20	*Rural N–20*
< 80	–	7
81-85	5	13
86-90	13	–
91-95	2	–
Total	**20**	**20**

It is very interesting to note that all the groups in the urban areas could be rated very high between 81-95 per cent total scores. On the other hand, only 13 out of the 20 groups in the rural area obtained above 81-90 per cent scores.

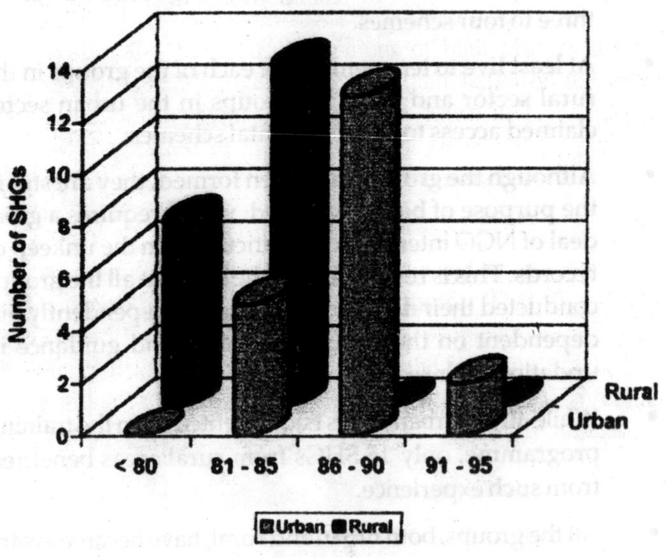

Fig. 6.5: Overall Rating of the SHGs

(III) Benefits Received from SHGs

Table—6.46 gives details regarding benefits derived by members from SHGs.

Table—6.46 Benefits derived by members from SHGs in the urban and rural areas

Benefits	*Urban (N : 358)*	*Rural (N : 357)*	*Total (N : 715)*
Habit of savings	340 (94.97)	330 (92.44)	670 (93.71)
Economic independence	284 (78.77)	112 (31.37)	222 (31.05)
Self confidence	254 (70.95)	282 (78.99)	536 (74.97)
Social cohesion	265 (74.02)	272 (76.19)	517 (72.31)
Asset ownership	292 (81.56)	145 (40.62)	437 (61.12)
Freedom from debt	320 (89.39)	315 (88.24)	635 (88.81)
Additional employment	120 (33.52)	125 (35.01)	245 (34.27)

Note: Figures given in brackets denotes percentage. Figures given in the column relate to multiple responses evinced by the respondents.

Benefits received include habit of saving (93.7 per cent), economic independence (31.05 per cent), self confidence (74.97 per cent), social cohesion (72.3 per cent), asset ownership (61.12 per cent), freedom from debt (88.81 per cent), additional employment (34.27 per cent). On the whole, SHGs have benefited their members in a variety of ways, triggering the developmental impulses among the downtrodden.

(B) Degree of Empowerment Traits Attained by the Micro Entrepreneurs

Empowerment entails struggle; it entails learning to deal with the forces of oppression, it entails having a vision of a new society; it also entails conscious and deliberate intervention and efforts to enhance the quality of life. Empowerment in this context entails gradually increasing control of poor women over the entire economic process and not merely as producers of some products and services which are otherwise controlled through other intermediaries. Transporting alien activities which do not have the long term regenerative and self-sustaining potential do not make the kind of activities that lead to empowerment. Thus, economic intervention is posited not only for enhanced income but also for increased empowerment of the poor women. A score card consisting of ten attributes was administered to the micro entrepreneurs of SHGs both at pre-credit and post-credit period.

Table—6.47 and Figure 6.6 shows the social changes evinced from the ventures undertaken by the micro entrepreneurs.

Table—6.47 Qualitative gains through micro credit

(Value in scores)

S. No.	Attributes	*Urban Block (N : 121)*				*Rural Block (N : 133)*			
		Mean score				*Mean score*			
		Base year	*Post credit year*	*Incremental Score*	*Percentage variation*	*Base year*	*Post credit year*	*Incremental Score*	*Percentage variation*
1.	Self confidence	2.07	7.23	5.16	249.28	1.97	6.47	5.30	452.99
2.	Hopes for better standard of living	2.60	7.64	5.04	193.85	1.92	6.99	5.07	264.06
3.	Better status in the family	1.82	5.99	4.17	229.12	2.33	5.45	3.12	133.91
4.	Communication skill	2.23	6.28	4.05	181.61	0.83	5.11	4.28	515.61
5.	Leadership	2.47	5.58	3.11	125.91	1.80	4.84	3.04	167.96
6.	Gained knowledge on credit management	2.44	5.99	3.55	145.49	1.50	5.38	3.88	258.67
7.	Good public relationship	2.36	7.89	5.53	234.32	2.59	7.52	4.93	190.34
8.	Economic independence	2.19	6.86	4.67	213.24	2.56	6.80	4.24	165.63
9.	Social cohesion	2.69	7.31	4.62	171.75	2.07	6.92	4.85	234.30
10.	Self expression—Decision making	2.15	7.89	5.74	266.98	2.11	7.97	5.86	277.73
	Total	**23.02**	**68.68**	**45.66**	**198.35**	**18.87**	**63.42**	**44.55**	**236.09**

It is to be noted that the mean incremental score of the members in the urban area for "self confidence" was 5.16 with 249.28 per cent variation. The mean incremental score in the rural area was found to be 5.30 with 452.99 per cent variation. The variation was more for the rural women when compared with urban women. This showed that the rural women had become more confident than the urban women. The improvement in self confidence might be due to the several opportunities given to the women to interact with the field staff, bank line departments, personnel and the opportunity for independent decision making.

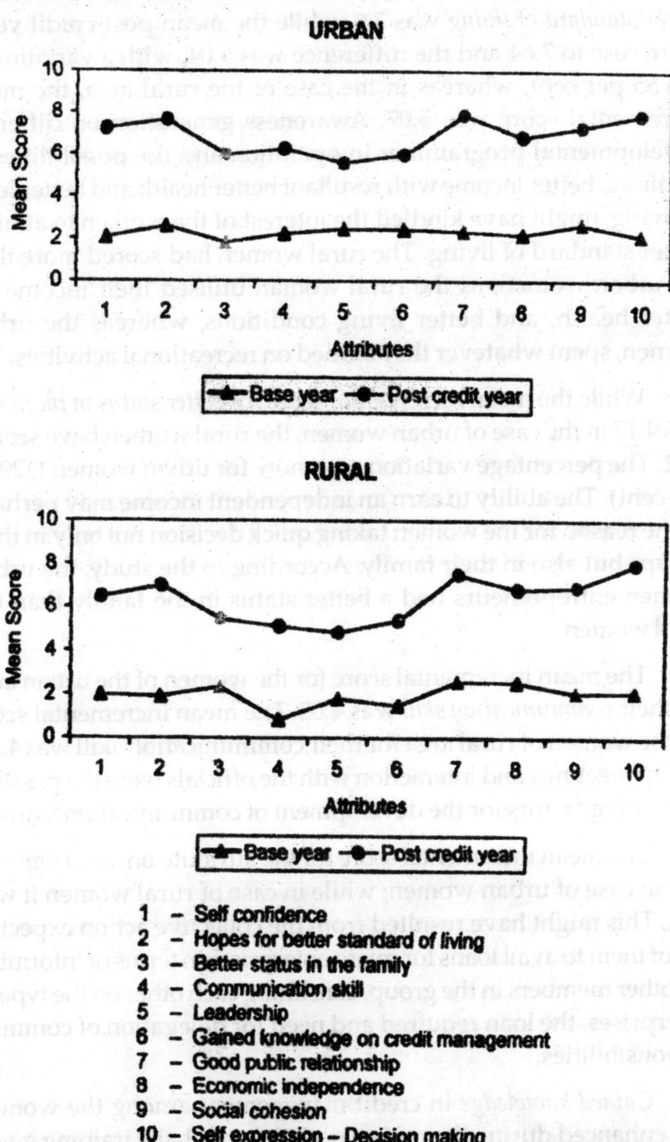

Fig. 6.6: Qualitative gains through micro credit

In the case of the urban area, the mean incremental score for *better standard of living* was 2.6, while the mean post-credit years score rose to 7.64 and the difference was 5.04, with a variation of 193.85 per cent, whereas in the case of the rural area, the mean incremental score was 5.07. Awareness generation on different developmental programmes in operation and the possibilities of obtaining better income with resultant better health and better level of living, might have kindled the interest of the women to attain a better standard of living. The rural women had scored more than the urban women, as the rural woman utilised their income for better health, and better living conditions, whereas the urban women, spent whatever they earned on recreational activities.

While the mean incremental score for *better status in the family* was 4.17 in the case of urban women, the rural women have scored 3.12. The percentage variation was more for urban women (229.12 per cent). The ability to earn an independent income may perhaps be the reason for the women taking quick decision not only in their groups but also in their family. According to the study, the urban women entrepreneurs had a better status in the family than the rural women.

The mean incremental score for the women of the urban area for their *communication skill* was 4.05. The mean incremental score for the women of rural area for their communication skill was 4.28. Group meetings and interaction with the officials were the possible facilitating factors for the development of communication skills.

The mean incremental score for the attribute on *leadership* was 3.11 in case of urban women; while in case of rural women it was 3.04. This might have resulted from the collective action expected out of them to avail loans for micro enterprises in terms of informing the other members in the group, consulting each other on the type of enterprises, the loan required and need for delegation of common responsibilities.

Gained knowledge in credit management among the women was enhanced during the project period through the training given on credit management by the investigator and the bank officials. This might have been the reason for a highly significant difference (3.55 in case of urban women, 3.88 in case of rural women).

Development of different traits would empower women in different dimensions and they would ultimately nurture a *good public relationship* as is evident from an increase in the mean score of this attribute by 5.53 and 4.93 for urban and rural women respectively, which were highly significant.

An increase of 4.67 for urban and 4.24 for rural women in the mean score for the attribute *economic independence*, which was a significant value, points out that the experience in initiating micro enterprises not only enabled the women to raise their household income but also made them to realise their own capabilities and instilled in them the positive thinking that given the impetus they would exercise the power within them and also enhance the same.

In case of urban women the incremental score for the attribute *Social cohesion* was 4.62 while that in case of rural women, the incremental score was 4.85. The improvement may mainly be attributed to opportunities provided to them to discuss the problems of each other in their own groups as well as in common meetings, exposure to the oppressions other women faced and the insistence of the co-ordination on the need for self help and mutual help through formation of SHGs and thrift and credit societies among themselves.

The mean incremental score for the trait *self expression* was 5.74 with 266.98 per cent variation in case of urban women whereas in case of rural women, it was 5.86 with 277.73 per cent variation. Opportunities to speak with in the group, with the officials concerned, participation in awareness campaign, enhanced income leading to greater control over resources at home and participation in infra family decision making on resource allocation and use might have contributed to the acquisition of this empowerment attribute.

(C) Problems in Implementing Micro Credit Programme

Many problems crop up at the operational level in implementing a poverty alleviation programme like micro credit. The various evaluation studies reviewed earlier highlighted the problems and issues that arose in the implementation of the programme. The basic objective of micro finance is to lift the poor women belonging to the weaker and backward sections of the rural society above the poverty line. The women in the groups face a number of problems in getting them identified, obtaining bank loans, processing and maintaining assets, marketing products and repaying the loans. In addition to such genuine problems which they are likely to face, the women resort to malpractices, mostly out of compulsion or circumstances, such as diversion of loans to other purposes, misuse of funds, etc. The problems encountered by the SHGs and the micro entrepreneurs in the study are analysed hereunder. The problems, as reported by the respondents, are presented in Tables—6.48 and 6.49.

Table—6.48 Problems faced by the self help groups in implementing micro credit programme

(Value in percentage)

S. No.	*Problems*	*Urban (% to total) (N : 20)*	*Rural (% to total) (N : 20)*
1.	Group conflict	60	40
2.	Inadequate bank linkage programme	90	60
3.	Inadequate networking	75	80
4.	Delay in execution of development programme	40	50
5.	Recovery of loans	50	60
6.	No training facilities	75	40
7.	General fear that the members will not make productive use of loans	40	50
8.	Members are not in regular in attending the group meeting	100	80
9.	No interest is shown by some of the members in taking decisions at the meeting	65	60
10.	Problems in electing and selecting the leader of the group	40	25

(Percentage given in the column relate to multiple responses evinced by the groups.)

Table—6.49 Problems faced by micro entrepreneurs

S. No.	Problems	Respondents in percentage	
		Urban (N : 121)	Rural (N : 133)
1.	Lack of awareness of the programme	37.19	56.39
2.	Lack of knowledge in identifying the product/trade—Selection of the product and trade	23.14	82.71
3.	Non-availability of infra structural facilities	67.77	27.07
4.	Amount of assistance inadequate	80.99	86.47
5.	Diversion and misuse of loans	51.24	43.61
6.	Lack of training in maintaining assets and utilisation of asset	56.20	47.37
7.	Inadequate supply of raw materials	19.00	33.83
8.	Inadequate marketing facilities	31.40	63.91
9.	No follow up and monitoring either by the NGO/banks	14.88	48.87
10.	High rate of interest charged by the group	61.16	75.94
11.	Male dominance in selecting and use of asset	66.12	84.21
12.	Financial stringency	78.51	51.13
13.	Social exclusion	24.79	26.32
14.	Traditional customs recognising the male hierarchy	21.49	26.32
15.	Gender viability to move out of their pre-unit and fetch facilities	29.75	58.75
16.	Inadequate training on credit management, maintenance of books and registers, skills upgradation, preparation of business plan.	53.72	67.67

(Percentage given in the column represents the multiple responses tendered by the respondents.)

Problems Faced by the SHGs

The Table—6.48 reveals that all the groups in the urban area (100 per cent) and 80 per cent of groups in the rural area are facing a problem of the members being irregular in attending the group meetings. Most of the SHGs expressed the view (90 per cent) that they had very few linkage programmes with the banks. Most of the SHGs (75 per cent in urban, 80 per cent in rural) are also facing the problem with inadequate training facilities and inadequate networking. Only a very few groups of both urban and rural areas have mentioned that they have the problem of electing the leader of the group. The SHGs expressed the view that the members do not have much interaction during elections at the meetings. Thus the constraints expressed by the SHG members are highly relevant and realistic. The women had been dormant for many years and hence they need radical changes in their aptitude and attitude which will be a slow process. But the SHGs have made remarkable progress in upholding the sentiments and life-style of women and gearing them towards positive changes.

Problems Faced by Micro-entrepreneurs

The problems faced by the entrepreneurs in undertaking micro enterprises is given in Table—6.49. Most of the women entrepreneurs (81 per cent in urban area and 86 per cent in rural area) have expressed the view that the amount of assistance was inadequate. In the rural area, 82.71 per cent of the members stated that they did not have much knowledge in identifying the enterprises. The rate of interest charged by the SHGs was said to be high, by as many as 61.6 per cent of the members in urban group and 75.94 per cent in the members in rural group. Diversion of loans to other purposes was resorted to in order to meet the economic exigencies arising out of personal circumstances. In the study area, it was gathered that 51.24 per cent of the members in urban groups and 43.61 per cent of the members in rural areas have misused the loans. In urban area 78.51 per cent and 51.13 per cent in rural areas have said that they are facing a problem of financial stringency, that is, interest for non-payment of interest, penalties and fines for not attending meetings and for irregular payment was imposed. It was also reported by 53.72 per cent of the women in urban area and 67.67 per cent of women in rural area that the training on credit management, maintenance of books and registers, preparation of business plan etc., was inadequate.

SECTION IV

Appraisal of the Strengths and Weaknesses of the SHGs in Management

To examine the prospects of SHGs in micro credit management the researcher organised an interaction meet with the members of the groups during the post-credit period. The researcher conducted two programmes one, at rural level and the other at urban level. In the urban and rural areas. 80 women representing 40 groups each were present. In the light of above discussion, the prospects of SHGs in micro-credit management could be broadly judged based on their strengths, weaknesses, opportunities and threats. SWOT analysis was carried out on eighty women representing all categories of the micro-enterprises initiated. SWOT analysis is a qualitative tool which by identifying the strengths, weakness, opportunities and threats to the SHGs makes an overall assessment of the performance of the groups. The responses were as follows:

Strengths	*No. of respondents*
1	2
• SHGs are self-sustainable system of community organisations free from government.	45
• Regular meetings of the group enable long lasting group relationship.	64
• Groups promoted by banks and NGOs and their guidance, training to the members of the group, teaching of basic accounting principles, etc., would help for better administration of the group.	25
• Social cohesion in the group and selection/election of the group leader in rotation give a sense of responsibility to each member of the group.	80
• Credit portfolio covering both consumption and production purposes helps to maintain labour productivity and income generating activities.	35
• No collateral securities are required at the individual level	62
• Less paper work and the sanction process is simplified	46
• Loan repayment mechanism is at the group level, hence better recovery performance.	80
• Financial deepening in terms of coverage is achieved through small savers and borrowers.	22

(Table Contd...)

1	2
• Capacity building efforts	15
• Quick return	10
Weaknesses	
• Limited scope for future growth in membership	80
• Loan portfolio is dominated by consumption loan and hence there is limited opportunity for income generating activities	45
• Misuse and diversion of funds	65
• Higher interest rate charged by the groups	35
• Penalties and fines imposed for delay payment	20
• Inadequate market facilities for the products	10
Opportunities	
• Women's groups exclusively dominate the SHGs, their empowerment both in economic and social fronts	70
• Opportunities for earnings through deposits and higher off-farm income opportunities improve their disposable income	55
• For the banks, SHGs are better intermediaries	40
• Wide opportunity for capacity building	25
• Networking with banks, NGOs, Government departments and marketing agencies	15
• Appropriate management expertise, technology and skill training for individual and collective enterprise	52
• Exposure to the outside world	10
• Health and social security	35
Threats	
• SHGs do not have any legal status	55
• Rapid expansion in the number of groups without monitoring by the NGOs and banks may lead to their poor functioning	64
• Repayment failure	10
• Large number of competitors	80
• Establishing a brand and quality product is difficult	70

Social cohesion and loan repayment mechanism at the group level were considered *major strengths* by SHG women followed by regular meetings of the group, no requirement of collateral securities, as the next important strength. Self-sustainability, continued guidance from banks and NGOs, credit portfolio covering both consumption and production purposes, simple procedure for availing loan, capacity building efforts and quick return have been declared as cross culturally validated qualities of SHGs. Women regarding social cohesion and loan repayment mechanism at the group level as their major strength hence, proves that these strengths gives a sense of responsibility to each member of the group and better recovery performance.

Limited scope for future growth was considered their major weakness. Misuse and diversion of funds was considered the second major weakness by the women. Loan portfolio is dominated by consumption loan and hence there is limited opportunity for income generating activities. The other weakness of the SHGs were, higher interest charged by the groups, penalties and finds imposed for delay payment and inadequate market facilities for the products.

Women seem to consider that what has to be provided for their upliftment in any incentive or assistance but just opportunity. The analysis of opportunities brought out that the women groups exclusively dominate the SHGs, their improvement both in economic and social fronts was one of the greatest opportunity particularly for women to participate in the mainstream of development activities. Skill related opportunities such as appropriate management expertise, technology and skill training for individual and collective enterprise were considered important by the women in manufacturing lines. Opportunities for earning through deposits and higher off-farm income opportunities improve their disposable income. The women felt that the SHGs are better intermediaries for the banks. The members have the opportunity to expose to outside world. The opportunity of being treated on par with males in the society, they are confident that they have health and social security in the society.

The main threats facing SHG women were competition from small and big units and difficult to establish a brand and quality product. One of the major threats is that the SHGs do not have legal status. Rapid expansion in the number of these groups without close monitoring by the sponsoring agencies may lead to their poor functioning. This is more so when they diversity their operations that need better management capabilities.

This analysis of SHG women revealed that the strengths and opportunities were higher in degree than weakness and threats. This is a positive indication that women in the SHGs are confident of overcoming the minor weaknesses and threats utilising the major strengths and opportunities that they possess. Based on the above SWOT analysis, the suggestions for the promotion of SHGs in micro credit management has been incorporated in the conclusion chapter.

Summary

Chapter 6 provides ample evidence of the fact that organisation of women in the form of SHGs has showed the seeds of economic and social empowerment of women.

The study analysed the socio-economic profile of the micro-entrepreneurs, impact on income, asset position and employment of the concerned. As regards the poverty alleviation of the SHG women, *only 15.36 per cent have genuinely crossed the poverty line*. An analysis of income mobility among the micro entrepreneurs disclosed that, due to initiation of the micro enterprises, *they have shifted from lower income brackets to higher income brackets*, thus indicating the positive impact of micro credit on SHG members. It is observed that out of the 254 SHG members, 11 members have repaid the loan in full and only one has not started repayment which indicated a satisfactory repayment performance.

The basic strategy adopted to promote empowerment of women through SHGs comprises in organising women SHGs at the village level around savings and rotational credit programmes using their own resources, facilitating regular interaction and exchange of information, linking SHGs with external credit source like banks, NGOs, etc., imparting skill training to the members to manage their credit and take decisions, linking SHGs with rural development programmes, *thus enabling the members to expand their investment capital and develop leadership qualities and self-confidence.*

Thus the micro credit programme evolved through the SHGs in the study area for collecting saving, consumption and productive credit at the individual and group level, initiating micro enterprises, *integrating social and economic goals among small groups has the potential not only for financial deepening in the rural and urban slum areas but also for the empowerment of women in particular.*

7

Summary and Conclusion

This action research was intended to realise the core principle of one of the developmental agendas namely "Helping people to help themselves" and to empower women through economic emancipation. Accordingly, 20 self help groups (SHGs) in the Coimbatore corporation slums (urban) and Karamadai panychayat union (rural) were formed with 15-20 members in each SHG.

A total of 254 members initiated micro enterprises. There were 12 categories of micro enterprises spread under four sectors, namely agriculture and allied, manufacturing, trading and servicing. Petty trades predominated the income generation activities both in urban and rural settings.

The impact of micro credit utilisation by the SHG members was evaluated in quantitative and qualitative dimensions. The findings of the study are summarised hereunder.

PERFORMANCE OF THE SHGs

Profile of the Members of the SHGs

- A total of 358 women from the urban and 357 women from the rural areas joined the SHGs.
- Hindu religion predominated both in the urban and rural areas under study.
- Scheduled caste members were in the majority (65.65 per cent) in the case of urban areas and backward castes (53.78 per cent) were prominent in rural areas.

- The families were mainly of the small sized unclear type, (1-4 members) reflecting the national trend.
- The majority of the group members belonged to the age group of 31-40 years both in the urban (52.79 per cent) and rural areas (58.82 per cent).
- Regarding educational status, 30.16 per cent women from urban areas and 40.61 per cent from rural areas were illiterate.
- Income-wise, 92.46 per cent from the urban slum and 97.76 per cent from the rural areas were below the poverty line.

Thrift and Credit Activities of the SHGs

- All the members stated that they formed as a group mainly to initiate income generation activities and asset creation efforts.
- When interrogated on the reasons for joining the SHGs, urge to save and accumulate money, as well as, easy access to loans were highlighted.
- The quantum saved was greater in the urban areas than in the rural areas. The monthly savings ranged from Rs. 30 to Rs. 50 per head.
- The majority of the groups both in urban and in rural (95 per cent) reached 100 per cent level of savings, which was highly remarkable.
- It was seen that income from own labour was the major source (78.74 per cent) towards their thrift contribution.

Credit Flow Realised

- Saving to the tune of Rs. 3,15,300 had been mobilised by the 20 urban SHGs. In contrast Rs. 2,03,820 was mobilised by the 20 rural groups. The amount saved by the individual SHGs was in proportion to the number of members and the duration of their functioning.
- A majority of the urban SHGs (45 per cent) had given above Rs. 30,000 as credit to its members and the rural

groups (60 per cent) had lent credit to its members ranging between Rs. 10,000-20,000.

- The pattern of credit demanded showed that 43.21 per cent of urban SHG members and 44.18 per cent of rural SHG members availed loan for income generation activities and 56.79 per cent for urban and 55.82 per cent for rural availed loan for other consumption and domestic purposes.
- As many as 280 women from urban areas and 301 women from the rural areas had benefited out of the internal lending, the loan amounts varying from Rs. 500 to Rs. 2000.
- Internal lending to the tune of Rs. 6,12,650 was reported in the urban areas. In the rural areas the internal lending was proportionately Rs. 3,36,400.
- Utilisation of credit had been of the order of 39.11 per cent of the internal lending utilised for income generation activities, 33.09 per cent for domestic consumption purposes and 12.17 per cent for family health.
- As for the thrift-credit ratio which is the crux of the SHGs, the urban SHGs had 1 : 1.94 while for the rural SHGs it was 1 : 1.65. The calculated 't' value showed that there was no significant difference between the areas in regarding percentage of mean credit to mean thrift in the SHGs.
- The loan repayment behaviour was satisfactory. In the urban areas, the recovery index was 100 per cent for 11 SHGs, 90-99 per cent for seven groups and 80-90 per cent for five groups; in the case of rural SHG groups the recovery index was 100 per cent for 19 groups and above 80 per cent for only one group.
- Statistical analysis revealed a high degree of correlation between the mean thrift, mean loan and the duration of the functioning of the SHGs.
- A majority of the SHGs (70 per cent) in the urban and (55 per cent) in the rural areas reported that they had 41-60 per cent of loans outstanding.

- The regression estimate of SHG net income per member both in the urban and rural areas on the plausible variables showed that increase in distance among members, higher education of the members, higher loan provided in the current year, lower SHG expenditure contributed to the higher SHG net income per month.

ECONOMIC RETURNS FROM MICRO ENTERPRISES UNDERTAKEN BY THE SHG MEMBERS

The economic impact from the micro enterprises undertaken by the SHG members on income, asset position and employment were analysed. This was preceded by a brief description of socio-economic characteristics of the micro entrepreneurs in the urban and rural areas such as size of families, age, occupational distribution, educational status, income levels, etc.

- Loan borrowed from SHGs was the highest (76.52 per cent) in the case of rural areas and those from the banks was the highest (58.51 per cent) in the case of urban areas. Dependence on moneylenders continued, in the case of 9.37 per cent of rural groups.
- A majority of the micro entrepreneurs, 31.40 per cent in urban areas and 34.58 per cent in rural areas, had made their investment in the micro project ranging from Rs. 1,001-2,000. This shows that the amount of credit needed by them remained small.

Income Generation

The primary objective of micro credit programme is to raise the income of the SHG member households by handing over to them a productive asset. Incremental income may enable the households to cross the poverty line or to move to a higher income group. The study revealed that the average household income of the micro entrepreneurs had increased by 53.62 per cent, representing Rs. 9,509.40.

- Area-wise analysis showed that the income generating effects of different areas were not the same. The incremental income of the SHG members in the urban area was relatively high (62.79 per cent) as compared to rural SHG members (46.19 per cent).

- Sector-wise analysis showed that the incremental income was as high as Rs. 5,085.27 (62.03 per cent) in the case of manufacturing sector. The servicing sector occupied the next place, recording an increase of Rs. 4,591.24 (51.87 per cent), while the agricultural sector had yielded the lowest incremental income of Rs. 3,872.61 (41.92 per cent). Cottage industry in the manufacturing sector yielded the highest incremental income of Rs. 5,893.91 (81.45 per cent), compared to all the other enterprises in all the sectors.
- Calculated 't' values, area-wise, sector and enterprise-wise, showed that the incremental income was statistically significant at one per cent level.
- The rate of return is referred to percentage of average income earned on average total investment made by the micro entrepreneurs. Area-wise analysis revealed that the rate of return was the highest (103.97) for urban entrepreneurs than for the rural entrepreneurs, as they could not maintain the asset to yield the maximum income.

The study revealed that taking all the enterprises together, the average income desired from micro credit programme was about Rs. 4,191.46, which followed from an average investment of Rs. 5,358.38. An analysis of enterprise-wise, investment income ratio showed that the rate of return was the highest (136.8 per cent) from cottage industries although the investment (Rs. 4,321.74) was lower. The rate of return on investment in the detergent-making enterprise was the lowest though, the investment was the highest. Diversion of assistance for other purposes might have been responsible for such a low rate of return.

ANOVA test revealed that the groups did not differ significantly in their average return on investment.

The multiple regression analysis results (Model I) showed that the average income of the entrepreneurs was influenced by the various sources of loan, such as SHGs, scheduled banks, corpus fund, friends and relatives, and moneylenders. The 't' value was 20.0792. This was taken area-wise and the sector-wise, the findings of the regression analysis showed that the estimated loan from SHGs led to an increase in the average income of the entrepreneurs. Therefore, to increase the income of the SHG members, it was necessary to increase the amount of loan for the members from their own SHGs for promoting micro enterprises by formulating appropriate credit policies for development.

The regression model II estimated results showed that the selected variables such as amount of loan, own funds, assets, employment, interest paid, household expenses, and the education of the members were relevant for explaining the variations in income of the member as the 't' value was 2.02361, which is significant as 5 per cent level. The co-efficient estimate showed that one rupee increase in the loan per member, own funds per member, value of assets per member and mandays per member, positively influenced the average income of the member.

The area-wise and sector-wise correlation analysis revealed that there was significant relationship between the investment and the income of the micro entrepreneurs. The enterprise-wise analysis showed that there was positive relationship between investment and the income of the entrepreneurs in the case of all the enterprises except petty shop and laundry business.

Shift of Household Above Poverty Line

The finding of the study was that out of 254 members, 25 members were above the poverty line in the base year. On the whole, out of 229 genuinely poor households, 39 households (15.36 per cent) crossed the poverty line. Among the sectors, manufacturing sector was more effective in alleviating poverty, followed by trading sector.

Shift of the Entrepreneurs to Higher Incomes

Using poverty line alone may amount to under-estimating the impact of micro credit management because the crossing of poverty line by the assisted families depends much on the pre-micro credit assistance family income.

Another shortcoming of taking poverty line alone as the criterion to judge the impact of micro credit management is that the duration of operation of the programmes is too short to produce the expected results. In view of these limitations, the income shifts of the members were considered as the more reasonable index for assessing the economic returns from micro enterprises undertaken by the SHG members.

The study revealed that the micro entrepreneurs had moved from lower income to higher income ranges in the post-credit period. The number of members in the two income ranges declined and consequently resulted in a rise in the higher income ranges.

Asset Position

The micro-credit programme might have an inter-alia impact in creating additional assets as a result of reinvestment of surplus derived from micro enterprises undertaken by the SHG members. It was observed that the coverage value of assets had increased by 311.96 per cent. Among the areas, urban group members possessed more assets in the post-credit period compared to the rural group members. Regarding the asset creation in terms of percentages among the groups, it was high for the urban group members. Sector-wise/enterprise-wise analysis revealed variations in all the enterprises. The statistical 't' value reveals that there is a positive impact of investment on assets. The regression analysis also showed that all the co-efficients of the investment on assets were positive. The correlation analysis showed that there was a positive relationship between the investment and asset position.

Employment Generation

The analysis on employment generation revealed that the average household employment had increased for members in all the schemes. Taking all the micro enterprises together, the average household employment had increased by 45.56 mandays, indicating 28.37 per cent increase in the post-credit year. Thus the study revealed that the majority of the micro enterprise had made some real impact in terms of increasing the employment significantly.

Repayment Performance

Repayment of loans availed from various sources according to the repayment schedules is absolutely essential for enabling the financial institutions to recycle their funds. The repayment performance is one of the indicators of sound micro-credit management. It was observed that 4.33 per cent of the members were regular in repayment and had fully repaid the amount before the due dates. Further, the study revealed that only one per cent of the members had not started repayment even beyond three years. The micro entrepreneurs belonging to the agricultural sector, as a whole, had faired better in repayment, i.e. 8.70 per cent had repaid in full and 78.26 per cent had repaid more than 50 per cent of the loan amount.

SOCIAL BENEFITS ACCRUED TO THE MEMBERS OF THE SHGs

Group Dynamics of SHGs

- All the 20 groups in the urban as well as rural areas were found to be homogeneous; 13 groups from the urban areas and 14 groups from the rural areas had 16 to 20 members each; 15 groups from the urban areas and five groups from the rural areas had mixed castes.
- All the 20 groups in the urban and rural areas functioned in the most democratic manner with three leaders each. All the groups had over 90 per cent attendance in the meetings.
- In 10 rural groups, the bye laws of SHGs were known to all the members whereas in eight out of the 20 groups, awareness on the bye laws was limited.
- The degree of participation in decision-making was high in the case of the urban areas compared to that in the rural areas, due to the time lag in the formation of SHGs.
- With regard to the collection of savings, 19 groups both in urban and rural areas, found it smooth sailing.
- All the groups in the urban and rural areas followed uniform criteria for internal lending which confirmed group cohesiveness.
- All the urban groups and 19 rural groups had agreed upon a high rate of interest in order to mobilise more monetary returns to help other members; the recovery index worked out to be 100 per cent in the case of 11 urban and 19 rural groups which is a positive trend indicating the integrity of the members.

- All the groups had learnt the correct procedure for documentation and reporting to a satisfactory level, owing to their exposure to the credit management training.
- The groups were given training on developmental inputs. As a consequence the members of all the groups in the urban areas and 15 groups in the rural areas were made aware of 5 to 10 developmental schemes, the SHGs required a lot of NGO intervention, particularly in maintaining and updating their records.
- As the groups both urban and rural had become aware of bank procedures and fornalities, at least to a fairly satisfactory level, owing to the creed to open and operate bank accounts.
- As for overall rating, all the groups in the urban areas could be treated very high. Out of the 20 rural groups, only 13 obtained above 81 per cent scores.
- SHG members perceived several benefits through their membership in SHGs such as habit of saving, economic independence, social recognition, employment and freedom from debt.

Extent of Acquisition of Traits Leading to Empowerment of Women

The qualitative gains as revealed by 254 women, indicated that women were in the process of attaining various attributes of empowerment, which would bear testimony to the positive outcomes of economic independence acquired by the women through undertaking micro enterprises and it is being proved that the women are really becoming "partners in development".

Problems Encountered

All the SHGs in the urban areas and 80 per cent of the SHGs in the rural areas stated that the members were irregular in attending the group meeting. Inadequate bank linkage programme, inadequate networking, lack of training facilities and group conflict were some of the problems faced by the majority of the SHGs.

Most of the entrepreneurs (81 per cent in urban area and 86 per cent in rural area) expressed the view that the amount of assistance was inadequate. A majority of the women in the rural area (82.71 per cent) stated that they lacked the knowledge for identifying the appropriate product.

A majority of the entrepreneurs also reported that the males dominated the selection and use of assets. It was observed that 51.24 per cent of the women in urban area and 43.61 per cent in rural area had misused loans by diverting them to other purposes. The other problems faced by the entrepreneurs were lack of awareness of the programme, non-availability of infrastructural facilities, lack of training in maintaining assets, inadequate supply of raw materials and marketing facilities, lack of follow up and monitoring, high rate of interest, social exclusion, gender viability and inadequate training on credit management and maintenance of books and registers.

Thus the problems stated are worthy of consideration, demanding immediate attention. Only scientific acumen is built in the financial culture, there will be sustainability in the group performance. There must be adequate co-ordination between the various line departments in taking the programme to rural and urban settings. There is not dearth in schemes/project/programme but they must be channelised to the right groups at right time Sin the right perspective. Follow up and feed back are imminetry missing which must be rectified.

From the preceding sections it is clear that the micro entrepreneurs and SHGs are facing a number of problems. The micro entrepreneurs should be properly and regularly supervised to identify the defects and bottleneck in promoting micro enterprises.

APPRAISAL OF THE STRENGTHS AND WEAKNESSES OF THE SHGs IN MICRO CREDIT MANAGEMENT

The prospects of the micro credit management in the SHGs could be broadly judged based on their strengths, weaknesses, opportunities and threats (SWOT).

- The basic strengths of SHGs in micro-credit management were self sustainable system of community organisation, social cohesion in the group, credit portfolio covering both consumption and production purposes, minimised paper work, loan repayment mechanism and quick return.

- One of the major weaknesses of the SHGs in managing micro credit was that they had a limited scope for future growth in membership. Secondly, the loan portfolio was dominated by consumption loan and so there was limited opportunity for income generating activities.
- Since women's groups exclusively dominate the SHGs, their empowerment, both in the economic and the social fronts is one of the greatest opportunities to participate in the mainstream of development activities.
- One of the major threats is that the SHGs do not have any legal status. Rapid expansion in the number of these groups without close monitoring by the NGO may lead to their poor functioning. This is more so, when they diversify their operations that need better management capabilities.

Thus the action research has brought to light perceptible changes in the working of the SHG. A large number of women had taken up income generation activities like manufacturing food items, running dairy and grocery shops and adopting agricultural activities. Consequently, family incomes had substantially increased. Apart from the economic changes, tremendous social changes were also evident in the project areas. Women began to command more respect, found due affection and a rightful place in the family. Their involvement in family decisions had been substaintially enhanced. As a group, women had gained more confidence and power. All these factors established the empowerment of women.

SUGGESTIONS

On the basis of the findings of the study the following suggestions have been made that would help to improve the function of the micro-credit management by the SHG members the grassroot level:

- The process of SHG formation has to be systematic, whether it is formed by a bank or an NGO. Due to their closeness to the people and flexibility of operations, the NGOs seem to be better equipped to undertake SHG formation.
- The savings habit must be encouraged as a value in itself and not just as a means of increasing the fund position of the group. It encourages the thrift habit and controls unnecessary consumption.
- Every group needs a policy on how to manage the savings of members who leave the group voluntarily or are asked to leave for some person.
- Income generating activity should be based on available local resources and a reasonably assured market with profits. Goods to be produced, should be either for local needs or to facilitate traditional manufacture.
- The NGOs should also provide some common services for procurement of raw materials, marketing/quality support.
- All groups should be helped to become autonomous in their working and should have their own systems and programmes.
- Institutional credit facilities must be extended to women to develop their managerial skill for prompt repayment consciousness.
- Micro credit should be used to meet the current demands of the poor women, whether these are for health, education or consumption purposes. This will lead to a gradual improvement in the quality of their life and will enable them to identify activities for economic betterment. In this process they will learn fiscal discipline and be ready to take on market-oriented economic activities.
- To empower women, it is necessary to make women equal partners in the national development process and equip them to make choices in order to actualise their self worth.

- Tremendous efforts are required for women's resource development in the spheres of education, health care, sanitation, food security, population education and domestic resource mobilisation.
- Periodic training programmes should be conducted not only for group leaders but also for the group members. To enhance the participation of all the members, exclusive membership education programmes need to be conducted.
- Potential members of old groups can be taken to visit the new groups to clarify various aspects of Self Help Group functioning.
- Able leaders from a few groups can be motivated to take up promotional and conflict resolution responsibilities. They can visit problematic/sick groups to explain and resolve various issues for smooth functioning.
- Training in book-keeping, accounts, fund management and other financial matters related to SHGs is essential to make the members competent enough to deal with the increasing volume of transaction.
- Annual Plans for SHG activities should be done by the group in consultation with the NGOs. The group leaders from different villages can meet once in a month and present the progress of their groups. Such review by all the groups will promote mutual learning.
- Exposure visits to relatively successful group ventures of other SHGs can be organised to share the knowledge, experience and expertise.
- Rapid expansion in the number of groups should be followed by a close and continuous monitoring of their health. This is very essential to prevent the groups losing their efficacy. An effective group monitoring system in the case of groups is a future challenge which should be met with by developing group structure like clusters and federations. With the expansion of groups and its

multiplier effect upon common fund, constant monitoring becomes very crucial and leaders need to be trained.

- The vertical structures and their management require capacity-building and promotion of leadership from the grassroots upwards within the SHG structure. But they should not be imposed from above.

IMPLICATION OF THE STUDY FOR FUTURE POLICY MAKING

The following are the recommendations which may be considered in future policy-making:

To the Government

- Create a positive financial regulatory framework that enables micro credit programme to accept savings deposits.
- Create autonomous national and sub-regional micro-credit funds, to help channel donors resources to micro credit NGOs with minimum Government intervention.
- Create favourable macro policies to reduce and eliminate obstacles that women face, in terms of property rights, inheritance laws and other discriminatory practices.
- It is desirable that Poverty Alleviation Programmes can be dove-tailed with SHGs so that effective implementation of the schemes will be possible through group approach. The SHGs are operating on the basis of mutual benefit societies and there is a probability that the interest income may attract income tax. Necessary amendment under the Income Tax Act completely exempting the interest income of SHGs should be made. The Stamp Act of the states does not exempt SHG lending from payment of stamp duty. As the members of SHGs belong to poorest of the poor category, State Government may be requested for amending the Stamp Act.
- Micro enterprise development of the poor under SHG framework underlines the need for a deliberate policy

frame in favour of assurance in terms of technology back up, product market and human resource development. However, in the context of economic liberalisation, there are indications that the markets are turning out to be unfriendly to the poor. Hence there is an urgent need to provide insurance for the products of micro enterprise sector through a suitable institutional mechanism.

- Micro credit movement has to be viewed from a long term perspective. Its mission goes beyond development through credit for poverty reduction. Micro-credit management by SHGs sows the seeds for a self-reliant economy incorporating certain business culture and social development action within the community as essential elements for economic and social mobility of the poor.
- Introduce special pension scheme for women by paying extra benefits to women to become independent in their old age.

To the Practitioners of Micro Credit

- Increase the use of cost-effective poverty measurements.
- Build more national, regional and global networks of micro finance institutions to increase the sharing of lessons learned and best practices.
- Ensure that women's empowerment is considered in all aspects of micro credit programme operations.
- There is need for a regulatory framework to standardise best practices and evolve rating norms for SHGs so that the SHG-Bank linkage programme could be firmly established.

To the Private Sector

- Create new and strategic partnerships between micro credit programmes and the private sector.
- Promote socially responsible investments that are pro-poor, pro-women and pro-environment.

To the NGOs

- Educate the public about the effectiveness of micro credits as an anti-poverty tool and about what individuals and organisation can do to make a difference.
- Continue to advocate the elimination of poverty and the fulfillment of international commitments.

Conclusion

This action research project established, that properly designed and effectively implemented micro-credit programme can not only alleviate poverty but also empower women at the grassroots. It proves that if development programmes are properly designed and sensitively implemented. The programme can become a key in unlocking the creative and productive potential of rural women. The SHGs which create a silent revolution must be viewed as 'change agents' in rural areas. As the illustrious Noeleen Heyzer, Co-chair UN Council, Micro Credit Summit, rightly pointed out, "Micro credit is much more than access to money. It is about women gaining control over the means to make a living. It is about women lifting themselves out of poverty and vulnerability. It is about women achieving economic and political empowerment within their homes, their villages, their countries". Thus promotion of income generation activities through micro credit among Self Help Group women, no doubt ensures their economic independence and social status.

Bibliography

Books

Adams Dale, W. and A. Delbert (1992), *Fitchett Informal Finance in Low Income Countries*, Oxford: Westview Press.

Aloysuis Prakash Fernandez, (1994). *The Myrada Experience: Alternate Management Systems for Savings and Credit of the Rural Poor*, Bangalore: The Mysore Resettlement and Development Agency.

Batliwala, Srilatha, (1994), "The Meaning of Empowerment New Concept from Action", In Adrienna Germain, Gita Sen and Lincoln Chen (eds.), *Population Policies Reconsidered: Health, Empowerment and Rights*, Cambridge, Macs: Harward School of Public Health.

Calman, Leslie, J. (1992), *Towards Empowerment: Women and Movement Policies in India*, New York: Westview Press.

Chen, Martha, A. (1996), (ed.) *Beyond Credit: A Subsector Approach to Promoting Women's Enterprises*, Canada, Ottawa: Aga Khan Foundation.

Ela Bhatt, (1997), "Women and Development Alternatives, Micro and Small Scale Enterprises in India" in (ed.). Louise, Dignard and Jose Hennet, *Women in Micro and Small Scale Enterprise Development*, San Fransico: Westview Press.

Gupta, R.C. (1994), *Management of Savings and Credit Programmes by NGOs*, New Delhi: Har-Anand Publications.

Gupta, S.P., (1996), *Statistical Methods*, New Delhi: Sultan Chand and Sons, pp. 3-9.

Hans, Dieter Siebel, (2000), "Agricultural Development Banks Close them on Reform them", *Finance and Development*, Washington, D.C. International Monetary Fund, pp. 45-47.

Howarth Rhona and Langdon Keren, (2000), *Organising Self Help Groups*, New Delhi: Department of Women and Child Development, Government of India.

Karmakar, K.G. (1999), *Rural Credit and Self Help Groups: Micro-Finance Needs and Concepts in India*. New Delhi: Sage Publications.

Kothari, C.R. (1994), *Research Methodology—Methods and Techniques*, New Delhi: Vishwa Prakashan, pp. 124 and 140.

Kuchhal, K.C. (1999), *Financial Management: An Analytical and Conceptual Approach*, Allahabad: Chaitanaya Publishing House, pp. 196-197.

Kulkarni, P.V. (1994), *Financial Management—A Conceptual Approach*, New Delhi: Himalaya Publishing House, pp. 456-457.

Manuja Devi, K. (1997), *Rural Women: Poverty Alleviation Programme*, New Delhi: Anmol Publications Pvt. Ltd.

Marilyn Carr, Martha Chen and Renana Jhabvala, (1996), *Speaking Out: Women's Economic Empowerment in South Asia*, New Delhi: Vistaar Publications.

Mullins, L.J. (1992), *Management and Organisational Behaviour*, London: Y.P. Chopra, p. 411.

Narasaiah Laxmi, M. and G. Jaya Raju, (1999), *Rural Development and Anti-poverty Programme*, New Delhi: Discovery Publishing House.

National Bank for Agriculture and Rural Development (NABARD), (1996), *International Seminar on Development of Rural Poor Through the Self Help Groups*, Bangalore: Development Policy Department.

Pillai, J.K. (1995), *Women and Empowerment*, New Delhi: Gyan Publishing House.

Prasad Kamta (2000), (eds.), *NGOs and Socio-Economic Development Opportunities*, New Delhi: Deep and Deep Publications Pvt. Ltd.

Quinones, Benjamin, R. (1992), *Self Help Groups as Informal Financial Intermediaries*, Bangkok: Asia Pacific Rural and Agricultural Credit Association.

Ridgeway, C.L. (1983), *The Dynamics of Small Groups*, New York: Martin Press.

Sekaran, Uma (1994), *Organisation Behaviour: Text and Cases*, New Delhi: Tata McGraw Hill Publishing Company Limited, p. 117.

Sen, Biswaji (1997), *From Self Help Groups to Community Banking*, Bangalore: The Pradhan Project for Empowerment of Women and Resource Centre.

Sinha Tara (2000), *Network of Self Help Groups*, New Delhi; Department of Women and Child Development, Government of India.

Srinivasan Girija, (2000), *Training of Self Help Groups*, New Delhi: Micro-credit Development Bureau.

Subramanian, K. and T.K. Velayudham (1997), (eds.), *Banking Reform in India—Managing Change*, New Delhi: Tata McGraw Hill Publishing Company Limited.

Sushma Sahay (1998), *Women and Empowerment: Approaches and Strategies*, New Delhi: Discovery Publishing House.

Suranjana Gupta (1998), *Visiting Alternatives on Inter State Study Tour on Savings and Credit*, Mumbai: Swamyam Shikshan Prayog.

Wilkinson, T.S. and P.L. Bhadarkar, (1982), *Methodology and Techniques of Social Research*, Mumbai: Himalaya Publishing House.

Young, K. (1988), *Gender and Development: A Rational Approach*, London: Oxford University.

Journals

Arora, Sukhwaider Singh and Mankad, Dhruv, "Banking on the Poor", *National Bank News Review*, 11 (2), April—June, 1995.

Besley, T. and S. Coate, "Group Lending, Repayment Incentives and Social Collateral", *Journal of Development Economics*, Vol. 46, No. 1, 1995, pp. 1-18.

Bhagalakshmi, "Environment of Women through Thrift and Credit Groups", *Gramvikas Newsletter*. Vol. 11, No. 3, June 1995, p. 18.

Bhatt, Ela, R. "Micro Insurance is Micro Finance", *The Economic Times*, July 31, Mumbai.

Desai, B.M., "Review of Book: A Study of SHGs and Linkage Programme", *Indian Journal of Agricultural Economics*, Vol. 55, No. 1, January-March, 2000.

Goetz, A.M. and R. Sen Gupta, "Who Takes the Credit? Gender, Power and Control Over Loan Use in Rural Credit Programmes in Bangladesh", *World Development*, Vol. 24, No. 1, 1996.

Gopalan Sarala, "Paradigm Shift from Welfare to Empowerment", *Social Welfare*, Vol. 43, No. 5, 1996, pp. 32-33.

Jain, R.K., "Economics Self-reliance for Women", *Social Welfare*, Vol. XL, No. 11-12, 1994, pp. 18-21.

Kausik, Amarchand, "Income Generation Effects of Rural Credit: A Case Study of IRDP in Haryana", *Journal of Rural Development*, Vol. 12, No. 1, 1993, pp. 89-102.

Khalkar, R.K., "Impact of IRDP on Income, Employment and Consumption Expenditure of Rural Poor in Mahendragarh District of Haryana State", *Journal of Rural Development*, Vol. 6, No. 5, 1987, pp. 475-485.

Koch, Eckart, "Linking Banks and Self Help Groups in Indonesia Experiences and Strategies", *Asia Pacific Rural Finance*, 5 (3), January-March, 1993.

Krishnaveni, L. and Sujma, A.L., "Women's Status—Does Employment Enhance Decision Making Power?" *Social Welfare*, Vol. 39, No. 9, 1992, p. 9.

Kumaran, "Self Help Groups: An Alternative to Institutional Credit to the Poor: A Case Study in Andhra Pradesh, *Journal of Rural Development*, 16 (3): 1997.

Lalitha, N., "Women's Empowerment through Co-operatives", *Social Welfare*, Vol. 43, No. 6, 1996, pp. 22-24.

Llanto, Gilberto. M., "Asymmetric Information in Rural Financial Markets and Interlinking of Transactions through the Self Help Groups", *Savings and Development*, Vol. 14, No. 2, 1990.

Manivannan, R., "Innovations in Rural Lending: Self Help Groups", *Indian Overseas Bank Monthly News Review*, 5 (6) June, 1992.

Misra, A., "Self Help Programme", *Tamilarasu Magazine of the Government of Tamil Nadu*, 1997, p. 11.

Misra, B., "Approach to the Ninth Plan: Need for Hard Decisions", *Kurukshetra*, Vol. XLV, 1997, pp. 17-18.

Mohan, R., "Major Revamp of Banking System Urge", *Business Line*, September 27, 1997.

Montogomery, Richard, "Disciplining or Protecting the Poor? Avoiding the Social Costs of Peer Group Pressure in Micro-credit Schemes", *Journal of International Development*, 8 : 2, 1996, pp. 289-305.

Parvathi, S., K. Chandrakandan, R. Ganeshan and C. Sekhar, "Economic Empowerment Needed", *Social Welfare*, Vol. 43, No. 1, 1996, p. 1.

Pathak, P.A., "Self Help Groups and their Linkages with Banks", *National Bank News Review*, Vol. 7 (II), 1992.

Paul, B., McGuire and D. John, "Conory Bank—NGO Linkages and the Transaction Costs of Lending to the Poor through Groups", *National Bank News Review*, October-December, 1997.

Pramod, B. "Developing Banking for the Poor: A Conceptual Framework", *Pigmy Economic Review*, Vol. 35 (II), June, 1990.

Prasad Hemalatha, C. and Prakashom, "Sustainable Employment for Women, Mahila Chetna Manch Shows the Way, *Gramin Vikas Newsletter*, June 1997, p. 13.

Rajasekar, D., Problems and Prospects of Group Lending in NGO Credit Programme in India", *Savings and Development*, Vol. 20, No. 1, 1996.

Rangarajan, C., "Banking with the Poor", *Reserve Bank of India Bulletin*, Vol. XLVIII, No. 2, February, 194.

Rangarajan, V., "Rural Banking—Lesson from the Past", *National Bank News Review*, July-September, 1995.

Shridharan, Damyanty, "Encourage Self Help Group," *Social Welfare*, Vol. 44, No. 7, October, 1997, pp. 33-34 and 39.

Srinivasan, Girija, "Reaching Credit to Rural Poor-I: Legal Hurdles on the Path of Self Help Groups", *Business Line*, Jan. 31, 1996.

Srinivasan, Girija, "Reaching Credit to Rural Poor—II: Legal Hurdles on the Path of Self Help Groups", *Business Line*, Feb. 7, 1996.

Stigliz, J.E., "Peer Monitoring and Credit Markets", *The World Bank Economic Review*, Vol. 4, No. 3, 1990.

Sudheer, G., "Small Group Approach", *Kurukshetra*, Vol. XLN, No. 3, December 12, pp. 51 and 52.

Sundaram, Rao, S. and G. Padmaja, "Self Help Groups in Tirupati", "*Social Welfare*, Vol. 45, No. 1, April, 1998, pp. 25-27.

Vasimalai, M.P., "Community Banking: Kalanjiam Way", *National Bank News Review*, Vol. 11 (4), October-December, 1995.

Veni, K.L., "Status of Indian Women", *Social Welfare*, Vol. 43, No. 10, 1997, pp. 24-27.

Viswanathan, Sujatha, "Grouping Women for Economic Empowerment", *Yojana*, Vol. XII, No. 6, March, 1997, pp. 37-39.

Yadav, A.V. Sangwan, B.L. Yadav and S. Gandhi, "Potential and Preference of Rural Women for Income Generating Activities", *Khadi Gramodyog*, 41 (11) August, 1995, pp. 538-541.

Zeller, M. "Determinants of Repayment Performance in Credit Groups: The Role of Programme Design, Intra-Group Risk Pooling and Social Cohesion", *Economic Development and Cultural Change*, Vol. 46, April, 1998, pp. 599-620.

Reports

Biswajit Sen, "From Self Help Groups to Community Banking", Bangalore: *The Pradhan Project for Empowerment of Women and Resource Centre*, 1997.

Brochures of NABARD, "Emerging Micro Finance Innovations", New Delhi: 1997, pp. 1-13.

Brochure of the Indonesian Movement for Micro Finance Development, Indonesia, 2000, A Network of Indonesian Micro Finance Actors for Poverty Alleviation.

Das, Maitreyi, "The Women's Development Programme in Rajasthan: A Case Study in Group Formation for Women's Development", Population and Human Resource Department, *The World Bank*, 1992, pp. 1-15.

Department of Women and Child Development, *Fourth World Conference on Women*, Country Paper, 1994, Beijing, New Delhi: 1995, p. 4.

Department of Women and Child Development, *Rashtriya Mahila Kosh: A Profile and Operational Guidelines*, New Delhi: 1996, pp. 1-2.

Department of Women and Child Development, *Annual Report*, Part-IV, New Delhi: 1996, pp. 49-51.

Department of Women and Child Development, *Rashtriya Mahila Kosh: Features of the Main and Sub-Schemes*, New Delhi: 1996, p. 5.

Department of Women and Child Development, *Workshop on Best Practices in Group Dynamics and Micro Credit*, New Delhi: February 15-17, 2000.

Gibbons David, S., "The Micro Credit Summits Challenge Working towards Institutional Financial Self-sufficiency while Maintaining a Commitment to Serving the Poorest Families", Paper Presented at *Micro Credit Summit Meeting of Councils in Abidjasi Cote d' Ivoire*: 24-27, June, 1999.

"Grameen Connections", *The Newsletter of Grameen Foundation*, Vol. 4, Issue No. 1, USA: 2000-2001, pp. 7-9.

Grameen Vikas Newsletter, *Ushering in a New Era of Women's Empowerment*, New Delhi: Vol. 13, No. 4, 1997, pp. 15-16.

International Fund for Agriculture and Development Policy on Rural Finance (IFAD), June 2000, pp. 16-17.

National Bank for Agriculture and Rural Development (NABARD), *Studies on Self Help Groups of the Rural Poor*, Mumbai: 1989.

National Institute of Bank Management, *Workshop on Linkages Between Self Help Group and Financing Institution*, Pune: 1991.

"Proceedings of First Meeting", *Indian Collective for Micro Finance*, New Delhi: 3-4, December, 1997, pp. 10-13.

Rashtriya Mahila Kosh, *Annual Report*, New Delhi: 1995, p. 1.

Reserve Bank of India, *Report on Trend and Progress of Banking in India*, 1997-98.

Susy Cheston, Larry Reed, "Measuring Transformation: Assessing and Improving the Impact of Micro-credit", Paper Presented at the *Micro Credit Summit Meeting of Councils in Abidjan, Cote d' Ivoire*: 24-26, June, pp. 11-15.

The Hindu, "Community Banking by Rural Women a Hit", September 20, 1998, p. 4.

The Indian Express, "Fatima B. Selected for UNDP's Race Against Poverty Award", Vol. LXVI, October 3, 1998.

United Nations, *The World's Women: Trends and Statistics*, New York: 1995.

United Nations Development Programme (UNDP), *The Human Development Report*, New York: Oxford University, 1995.

United Nations Development Programme (UNDP), *Annual Report*: Enduing Poverty and Building Peace through Sustainable Human Development, New York: 1996-97, p. 7.

Zeller, Manfrad and Manohar Sharma, "Rural Finance and Poverty Alleviation", *Food Policy Report*, International Food Policy Research Institute, Washington, D.C.: 1998.

Index

K

L

M

N

O

P

T

U

V

W

Methodology

(iii) Regression Analysis

Multiple Regression Analysis